HYBRID ACTORS

A CENTURY FOUNDATION BOOK

HYBRID ACTORS

ARMED GROUPS AND STATE FRAGMENTATION IN THE MIDDLE EAST

Thanassis Cambanis, Dina Esfandiary, Sima Ghaddar,
Michael Wahid Hanna, Aron Lund, and Renad Mansour

The Century Foundation Press
New York

About The Century Foundation

The Century Foundation is a progressive, nonpartisan think tank that seeks to foster opportunity, reduce inequality, and promote security at home and abroad. Founded in 1919 by the progressive business leader Edward A. Filene, The Century Foundation is one of the oldest public policy research institutes in the country. Over the past century, our experts have helped make the economy stronger, elections fairer, health care more affordable, and schools and society more equitable.

Library of Congress Cataloguing-in-Publication Data Available from the publisher upon request.

Manufactured in the United States of America
Cover design by Jonnea Herman
Text design by Cynthia Stock

Contents

Acknowledgments

This project would not have been possible without the generous support of Vartan Gregorian and Hillary Wiesner at the Carnegie Corporation of New York, which has enabled this multiyear effort. It was also made possible by the board of trustees and our colleagues at The Century Foundation (TCF), led by Chairman Bradley Abelow and President Mark Zuckerman. They have afforded us the time and space to continue TCF's commitment to international policy research. We are indebted to our foreign policy associates Rohan Advani, Abeer Pamuk, Lily Hindy, and Zeead Yaghi, who have supported this project at various stages. Project editor Eamon Kircher-Allen was, as always, thorough and indispensable. The TCF editorial team displayed their typical diligence and thoughtfulness in helping us with this work. We owe special thanks at TCF to Jason Renker and Abby Grimshaw. The authors would like to thank Renad Mansour for taking the lead in establishing the conceptual framework for the report. This report has benefited from the valuable insights of many peers, including Kheder Khaddour, Yezid Sayigh, Peter Salisbury, and Toby Dodge. We owe a special debt of gratitude to the trailblazing scholarship of Faleh A. Jabar. Responsibility for any errors rests with the authors alone.

Executive Summary

The fragmentation of the state in the Middle East and North Africa has become an increasingly urgent topic of study, as so-called nonstate actors have proliferated across the region in the past two decades. From Libya to Lebanon, Syria, Iraq, Yemen, and beyond, countless militias, parties, "brigades," "forces," "battalions," and "detachments" have emerged to directly challenge the formal state's hegemony over legitimate violence. These groups' emergence signifies more than simply a region beset by civil conflict and insurgency. It is also the result of a change in the political superstructure. The state is being challenged for its primacy as a political unit.

These new realities of the Middle East have stretched the existing nomenclature to its limits. The term "nonstate actors" is simply too large a basket to hold these diverse types of armed groups. Today, there is a need for more precise terms and categories, for policymakers and for those who study conflict and armed groups. In zones of eroded state authority, armed movements have played a transformative role. Some are simply shadowy arms of the state, even when they are designed to operate as if they were autonomous groups. Others are classic proxies, militias set up by a sponsor government, which operate with a veneer of independence but are in fact wholly controlled by their sponsor and serve their sponsor's policy aims.

This report is concerned with a third category: the hybrid actor, a type of armed group that sometimes operates in concert with the state and sometimes competes with it. Hybrid actors depend on state sponsorship and benefit from the tools and prerogatives of state power, but at the same time enjoy the flexibility that comes with *not* being the state. Hybrid actors seek to harness and control some but not all spheres of the state's authority. Those that survive over many years tend to penetrate the state and carve out official fiefdoms within its architecture. They engage in war, diplomacy, politics, and propaganda. They build and maintain constituencies, providing not just security but also services and ideological guidance. Though almost all hybrid actors have some relationship with an external patron, they are more than mere proxies, and have some latitude to make their own policies and decisions.

This report analyzes hybrid actors along two vectors: their "stateness" (the extent to which they seek to assume state functions) and their autonomy (the degree to which they function as proxies subservient to their patron). Part I develops the concept of the hybrid actor in more detail, situating it in existing theory. Part II presents seven case studies of armed groups and movements: The Popular Mobilization Units (PMU) of Iraq, Hezbollah of Lebanon, the National Defence Forces of Syria, Amal of Lebanon, the Kurdish parties of Iraq, the Iraqi Awakening, and the Islamic State. Some of these cases fully meet the definition of a hybrid actor; others fall short of it, but still exhibit some hybrid traits. Taken together, the case studies flesh out our understanding of the hybrid actor concept. Part III investigates the role of state sponsorship in the creation and evolution of hybrid actors, focusing especially on the case of Iran, which has enjoyed singular success in partnering with such groups. Part IV concludes with recommendations for how policymakers can draw on the hybrid concept to enhance rule of law, incorporate hybrid actors into state and other institutional and legal frameworks, and design more realistic strategies to support weak states in conflict zones.

Hybrid actors have established themselves as an enduring feature of the landscape in the Middle East and North Africa, and may be the single greatest impediment to the reconstitution of state authority. This report seeks to deepen our understanding of such groups and their relationship with weak states—and thus illuminate options for policies that will bring more peace and stability.

Introduction

Decades after their decisive arrival on the scene in the Middle East and North Africa, nonstate actors continue to confound policymakers, diplomats, and analysts. Today, we have clearer definitions and analytical frameworks that allow us to distinguish between nonstate proxy actors, which operate under the control of a sponsor while allowing plausible deniability, and hybrid actors, which develop domestic support by building a local constituency. Both types of actors may attract external sponsorship, usually from a state, and profess a distinct ideological identity. But hybrid actors are distinct in the way that they not only serve a security function, but also play a role in politics and economics—that is, hybrid actors assume some of the functions and autonomy of a state.

Others have produced comprehensive surveys of armed groups and have created taxonomies.[1] In this report, we are specifically interested in armed groups that have acquired enduring political and military significance by creating constituencies, while holding territory and engaging in armed conflict. The most important of these groups often capture state institutions and participate, to varying extents, in formal governance. However, these groups also develop structures parallel to the state, affording them extralegal autonomy. These hybrid groups engage in war, diplomacy, politics, propaganda, and constituency building. They are not states as such, and yet they manage long-term relationships with states, and in many cases shape their host states through symbiotic or combative relationships. This report analyzes hybrid actors along two vectors: their "stateness" (the extent to which they seek to assume state functions) and their autonomy (the degree to which they function as proxies subservient to their patron).[2]

Hybrid actors are powerful but difficult to define; as a result, analysts and policymakers often overlook them or mistakenly consider them to be something they are not, typically a state institution or a classic proxy. The emergence of hybrid actors is a worldwide phenomenon of conflict zones from Colombia to Libya to the Democratic Republic of Congo to Southeast Asia. At the current historical moment, hybrid actors are most prominent in the Levant, an intensely contested region. Several factors have contributed to the vast number of experiments by and with hybrid actors, as defined here, as well as with other proxies and militias: eroded state structures and institutions; open-ended civil and regional wars; sustained interference by competing foreign powers; the resource curse; and the instrumentalization of identity and ideology by local elites. Interventionist powers continue to support nonstate actors and hybrids, sometimes in opposition to states, sometimes as hedges against states that they also support, and at other times as an expedient option to accomplish policy goals. Recent conflicts in Syria, Iraq, Yemen, and Libya all feature foreign intervention on behalf of hybrids—even by governments that also are allied with the state in question. Hybrids thrive where the state is weak and interventionary powers tolerate or even prefer dynamic instability to central authority. At present, Iran is the power most heavily invested in hybrid actors—in part as an ideological function of its revisionist and revolutionary agenda, and in part as a practical function of its limited options for both power projection and state-to-state partnerships in the Middle East and North Africa. Competitor powers in the region, including Israel, the United States, and the Arab states of the Gulf, have all engaged with proxies and hybrids. However, these competitor powers face structural constraints that have limited or undermined their ability to cultivate effective and sustainable partnerships with such groups.

This report identifies some of the key conditions that have made certain hybrid actors successful and persistent, including constituency cultivation, secure relations with their host state, and steady foreign support. Hybrids have assumed geopolitical significance, and are likely to have a wide range of effects across the myriad underlying policy interests that shape the region and its conflicts. If we are to understand the forces at play in conflict zones and design policy responses to those conflicts, we must understand hybrid actors and the ways in which they differ from states and other non-state actors.

Hybrid actors are pivotal drivers of conflict, insecurity, and the governance challenges that hobble the Middle East and North Africa. In many cases, hybrid actors arose in response to state failures to provide security or services. Today, those same actors, now mature, are a primary obstacle to state efforts to reestablish authority. In this sense, hybrid actors are both a symptom and a driver of state fragility, poor governance, and insecurity.

This report examines cases in Lebanon, Syria, and Iraq because these countries have seen a proliferation of armed groups and disproportionate investment by outside governments. Their conflicts have played host to classic proxies, pretenders to state power, and enduring hybrid actors. A closer look at these cases allows us to pinpoint the distinctions between these categories, and the ways in which some groups evolve along that spectrum. We measure a group's "success" according to its longevity, influence, and ability to project power militarily as well as politically. We also explore types of autonomy, evaluating the varying abilities of proxy or sponsored groups to deviate from their sponsor's orders. We believe the evidence from repeated experience with hybrid actors (and comparisons to other types of militias, armed groups, and pretenders to statehood) suggests the conditions that correlate with success for hybrid groups: constituent loyalty; resilient state relationships, including with sponsors; and coherent ideology, in the most compelling examples converging with that of their sponsors. We also believe that descriptive rigor makes it easier to distinguish between hybrid actors (such as Lebanon's Hezbollah), classic nonstate proxies (such as Iraq's Kata'eb

Hezbollah), and aspirants to statehood that seek to fully destroy the existing state and fashion a radically new one (like the Islamic State). All merit different analytical and policy treatment. This report does not intend to be exhaustive; however, it uses case studies from Iraq, Syria, and Lebanon to present the relationships of actors at three different levels: with their constituents; with their host states; and with the international system, including states and nonstate actors beyond the borders of their host state.

This report concentrates disproportionately on hybrid actors supported by Iran, because such groups currently are preeminent in the region. Such a focus helps us systematically unpack this useful new concept. Compelling cases in Iraq, Syria, and Lebanon allow us to refine the concept of the hybrid actor and show how its various forms can change how policymakers understand armed groups. We believe the hybrid actor concept can be applied to other cases—to groups in Syria like Tahrir al-Sham (formerly known as the Nusra Front) and other Sunni armed opposition groups, and the Kurdish People's Protection Units (known by its Kurdish initials, the YPG [Yekîneyên Parastina Gel]). It also can be applied to state sponsors of nonstate and hybrid groups, including Turkey, Qatar, Saudi Arabia, and the United States, and to regions beyond the Middle East and North Africa.

The range of examples in these case studies highlight recent relevant facets of hybrid actors. Some illustrate the pathways to establishing successful hybrid groups, and others show the ways in which potential hybrid actors evolve beyond hybridity or fall short of that level. They also present the ways in which consequential nonstate actors fail to meet the criteria for hybridity. In Lebanon, for example, the experience of the political party Amal can be compared to that of Hezbollah. Both groups emerged decades ago as militias, but Amal has grown into being a traditional political actor, whereas Hezbollah has become a true hybrid actor. Although the two groups arose in similar circumstances, their trajectory reflects the variable pressures and influences that can produce distinct results, including moving beyond hybridity and into formalized political life.

This report seeks to illuminate the ways in which influential armed actors can amass power and then project it through, with, and against the weak states in which they arise. Hybrid actors, after all, are not simply proxies or nonstate groups. Understanding their distinctive outside-in approach to the state is critical to understanding power relations within weak states and the ways in which policy responses to them should be formulated.

I. The Hybrid Actor Concept

An overweening focus on the state as a unit of analysis has overshadowed another important force: the hybrid actor. Since at least the late Cold War period, policymakers and academics have acknowledged the importance of "nonstate actors," a loosely defined category that included multinational corporations, terrorist groups, criminal syndicates, liberation movements, and many other types of entities. Nonstate actors have grown in importance, in some areas surpassing weak states in authority. But in certain contexts, "nonstate actor" is not a meaningful label for the myriad entities the term sought to describe. The current political environment requires more discerning and precise terms to categorize a broad spectrum of actors.

In zones of eroded state authority, armed movements have played a leading and transformative role. Some are simply shadowy arms of the state, even when they are designed to operate as if they were autonomous groups. Examples of such stealth state bodies include the Fedayeen Saddam, an Iraqi paramilitary group from the Saddam Hussein era; the various Syrian progovernment militias, including some of the groups working under the National Defence Forces umbrella; and Russian operatives, disguised as local militias, deployed in former Soviet republics. Others are classic proxies—militias set up by a sponsor government, which operate with a veneer of independence but are in fact wholly controlled by their sponsor and serve their sponsor's policy aims.

This report is concerned with a third category: the hybrid actor, a type of armed group that sometimes operates in concert with the state and sometimes competes with it.[3] Hybrid actors depend on state sponsorship and benefit from the tools and prerogatives of state power, but at the same time they enjoy the flexibility that comes with *not* being the state and *not* being responsible for governance. Hybrid actors seek to harness and control some but not all spheres of the state's authority. Those that survive over many years tend to penetrate the state and carve out official fiefdoms within its architecture. Hybrid actors cannot be understood merely as proxies, or as militias. They have established themselves as an enduring feature of the landscape in the Middle East and North Africa, and may be the single greatest impediment to the reconstitution of state authority.

Any meaningful understanding of politics and security depends on a clear understanding of the physical world in which policy is exercised. Today, the state system is a woefully inadequate construct for analysis and policymaking, since it overlooks the entire spectrum of hybrid actors. To be sure, states are and continue to be important, but as a unit of analysis they do not tell the whole story. Those who study the state system have made well-intended but incomplete efforts to account for the transformed reality in conflict zones. Since the 1990s, Western policymakers have focused on fragile and failed states, which they perceive to be the root of conflict and humanitarian disaster in the Middle East and North Africa. They argue that these "failed," "failing," or "fragile" states are national security threats and represent instability in the region. In 2004, for instance, U.S. secretary of state Colin Powell formed the Office of the Coordinator for Reconstruction and Stabilization, which was intended to support Washington's ability "to respond to crises involving failing, failed, and post-conflict states and complex emergencies."[4] For international policymakers, then, state-building is a form of political intervention aimed at upholding de jure states (those with an internationally recognized legal basis) with an eye to preserving international peace and security. At times, however, this approach is at odds with new realities on the ground, where armed actors challenge internationally recognized governments.

To understand the emergence of state, nonstate, and hybrid actors, we must first define the state, which remains a contested concept. The seminal definition of the state that guides policymakers interacting in the Middle East and North Africa comes from German sociologist Max Weber, who defined the state as a fixed territorial entity, ruled by a central authority that has a monopoly over the legitimate means of violence.[5] The British sociologist Michael Mann adds that the state cannot only include despotic power (over society), but must also include infrastructural power, which he defines as "a cooperative relationship between state and society."[6] American scholar Charles Tilly adds other criteria to his definition: that the state must be able to go to war, to remove internal strife, to protect the population, and to collect taxes.[7] In Tilly's model of the state, the relationship between citizen and ruler is a transactional social contract in which protection is exchanged for taxation. To add a legal perspective, the 1933 Montevideo Convention on the Rights and Duties of States—a foundational treaty in modern international law—defines a state as any entity with a permanent population, a defined territory, a government, and the capacity to enter into relations with other states. All these authors and documents, in different ways, perceive the state as an empirical entity—a political system whose existence is self-evident. As a practical matter, a state can be said to exist simply by exhibiting the features of the definition.

However, Western state-building efforts since World War II have moved away from these definitions and focused more on international recognition as a prerequisite for statehood. Under this trend, policymakers today prefer to keep failing or failed states (in other words, entities that lack the abovementioned empirical criteria) on life support rather than to recognize new entities on the ground.[8] Yet a growing number of internationally recognized de jure states with formal borders and governments lack empirical statehood, or the capacity to implement the most basic functions of governance. This type of actor is what political scientist Robert Jackson calls a "quasi-state."[9] Such entities have the juridical features of a state—flags, national anthems, and United Nations membership—but not the empirical qualities described above. Quasi-states are stuck in a game of dependence upon external support structures, or top-down legitimization. They lack the "positive sovereignty" needed to be masters of their own fate or the "negative sovereignty" needed to be free from external interference. In these states, actual authority in a territory has fragmented, even as that territory nominally remains a state under international law.

Often, nonstate actors have filled the vacuum caused by the retreat of quasi states. Nonstate actors perform state-like functions and enjoy the empirical habits of statehood, but lack de jure recognition. In countries across the Middle East and North Africa, political opposition networks, local communities, and identity groups (including, for example, Salafi and jihadist groups) provide basic services that existing states have failed to supply. The lines between the formal and informal are blurred because there is a gap between de facto realities and what is established under law.[10]

International policymakers' insistence on supporting quasi-states and refusal to fully support nonstate actors (other than in temporary moments of convenience, such as with the People's Protection Units, or the YPG, in Syria) has stalled transformations. In the past, warlords who achieved de facto authority over a territory and expressed an interest in forming a state could become a state, without the need for juridical recognition. This process no longer exists. Today, nonstate groups—whose transition to states the international system has stalled—may serve as a lasting feature. Some of the actors within this political order even perform state-like functions, but are not recognized under international law. Instead, they become hybrid actors.

Armed Nonstate Actors

When defining the concept of states, international policymakers who focus on the Middle East often cite part of the Weberian logic that rests on the notion of monopoly over legitimate violence. However, as Mann wrote, "most historic states have not possessed a monopoly of organized military force and many have not even claimed it."[11] Such an absence of a monopoly on force has persisted in the Middle East and North Africa. Scholar Yezid Sayigh argues that there is a clear pattern of duality or multiplicity of "legitimate" or state-recognized armed actors, which is part of the deeper processes underway in affected Arab states. In more stable states, the multiplicity of armed actors is a lasting feature that emerged from an original political settlement that formalized militias into the state structure. One such formalized entity is Iran's Islamic Revolutionary Guard Corps (IRGC), created by Ayatollah Ruholla Khomeini in 1979 to consolidate the paramilitary groups loyal to the Islamic revolution as a counter to the regular military, which had been loyal to the shah. The Iranian state, after the revolution, would then consist of the traditional military (the Artesh)—which included the ground forces, the navy, the air force, and the air defense force—with its own command structure and joint staff—as well as the IRGC. Although the IRGC would become more powerful than the traditional military, legitimate violence was not centralized.

In states marred by stalled transformation where a political settlement has not yet been achieved—such as Iraq, Syria, Libya, Lebanon, and Yemen—a duopoly on the use of force, or competition between multiple actors, reflects the weakness of the unitary state, the decline of the social contract, and to some extent the erosion of national identity. In these countries, the de jure actors are not the only entities providing for the needs of a population or claiming to represent a population. Instead, a variety of nonstate entities and actors emerge to fill in for the receding state, and take de facto authority away from the de jure actors. The real-world distribution of power and force far exceeds any framework defined solely by the state.

Criminals, Insurgents, and Warlords

In many areas of the Middle East, the unitary state has retreated to the point where nonstate armed actors have supplanted their authority.

The literature traditionally has divided these actors into three distinct categories: criminal organizations, insurgents (or terrorists), and warlords (or militias). All three types of actors use actual or threatened violence to achieve their aims. The differences lie in their ultimate objectives. Criminal organizations and gangs evade or break the law for financial (but not political) gains. Insurgent groups, at times also referred to as terrorist organizations, use violence for political ends, by challenging the existence of the state in pursuit of a new legal order.

Warlords, by contrast, do not threaten to take over the state, nor do they seek to merely exploit the collapse of legal authority for monetary gain.[12] Instead, they are more interested in their own local governance model. Warlords, whether in antiquity or modern times, are charismatic leaders who operate in areas where the state's capabilities and legitimacy do not extend. The warlord wields some degree of political power, but also pays allegiance to the state or other stronger powers, in return for being left alone to govern his constituents in the periphery.[13]

Local communities have their own reasons for supporting warlords in place of the unitary state. In the context of violence or recent violence or the threat of violence, local populations value security above all, and consent to the actor who can protect them or move them away from violence. Warlords promote themselves as the most reliable protectors of their local communities from external threats, including the state. Another way that warlords develop their constituencies is by using ideological markers, such as religion, ethnicity, or sectarianism, to tie their communities together and to gain legitimacy within their chosen group. That said, most warlords restrict their ambitions to local power, even if they have a coherent ideology or social engineering project. By providing employment or even basic services for their constituencies when the state is no longer able to do so, they are able to secure the support of their local power base in the face of potential opponents.

Over the centuries, observers have noted that at a certain point, warlords may gain enough power to allow them to transform from locally and economically minded strongmen to become—or strive to become—a state actor.[14] In the Arab world, the thirteenth-century sociologist Ibn Khaldun noted that tribes that developed a strong sense of common purpose (what Ibn Khaldun called "asabiyya") eventually were able to conquer and take over the state. Although different from a tribe, authors often have argued that warlords operating in the environment of a weaker state will, similarly, at some point challenge for the state.[15] Most states, after all, are initially created by armed leaders who turn into statespeople.

These observations about the development of warlords give some insight into how modern hybrid actors emerge. Many hybrid actors begin first as warlords who provide security and basic services for their constituents at a local level. Their access to arms and ability to mobilize fighters allow them to solidify their position. Their fighters join for both ideological and economic reasons. Ideological motivations are often based on ethnicity or sect, and relate to a fight against an external threat. Economic motivations include gaining employment, such as at checkpoints, which warlords use to outsource labor costs and build patronage. Some armed actors go even further, building social networks of organizations that provide services and build constituencies.

A Change in the Relationship with the State

The forces of a warlord—or an armed group with a different kind of leadership structure that functions as a warlord—transform into a hybrid actor when the group begins to express a more national mandate and interest in the state. Prior to this point, the warlord's group provides services and protection, including protecting his community from the state. But at some point, the group becomes interested in the state for economic, geostrategic, ideological, and historical reasons. This process manifests in varying forms.

Foreign support for leaders in Middle Eastern capitals has stifled politics and foreclosed transformations. As a result, in many cases warlords are unable to fully transition into state actors. They cannot take over the government, nor, in some cases, openly join it. As a result, many such warlords evolve into hybrid actors. The hybrid actor thus represents a space between the locally minded warlord and the formal state actor.

Transforming into a hybrid actor, a group that once represented a warlord marks itself not only as the protector of a local community but also as the protector of the state itself. In Iraq, for instance, tens of predominantly Shia militias rose up in 2014 to fight against the so-called Islamic State in Sunni areas of the country. In this capacity, these warlords fought on behalf of the state, which faced an existential threat from the self-styled caliphate of the Islamic State that occupied up to one-third of Iraq's territory. In Lebanon, Hezbollah has similarly marked itself as the only reliable protector of the state, even though it exists beyond state control. In times of conflict, the ability to provide security becomes an important marker of the hybrid actor.

When the hybrid actor is unable to take over the state, it begins to develop different mechanisms to maintain its capability, legitimacy, and power, even without full integration. This process includes keeping one foot in the state and one foot outside it. At times, the hybrid actor cooperates with state authorities; at other times, it competes with the state for legitimacy, capability, and ultimately, power. Hybrid actors seek both to build local structures that run parallel to those of the weakened state *and* to gain a footing within the state.[16]

At some point, hybrid actors may desire to become participants in the state, for two primary reasons. First, in the context of many countries in the Middle East and North Africa, the state represents resources, particularly in rentier states. Control over a government ministry or agency (and its coffers) is financially rewarding. Second, the state also imparts a sense of legitimacy. In public opinion polls conducted across the region, respondents often claim that they would prefer to be ruled by government or state authority than by a nonstate actor.[17]

To gain more state power, hybrid actors often develop formal political parties that compete in local and national elections. For instance, in the 2018 Iraqi elections, the PMU formed an electoral bloc, the Fatah Alliance (also known as the Conquest Alliance), and placed second. Fatah's leader was Hadi al-Amiri, the long-time head of the Badr Brigades paramilitary group. Only Muqtada al-Sadr's coalition, Sa'iroun, placed ahead of Ameri in the elections. Sadr also controls a paramilitary group called the Peace Brigades (in Arabic, Saraya al-Salam). These paramilitary armed actors and their organizations ran in the elections, and then worked together to form the new government. Electoral success gave them more capital to send their proxies into government positions and thus to benefit from the wealth, legitimacy, and power associated with the state. Similar trends can be found in other countries of the region, where armed actors seek a slice of the national pie.[18] Ultimately, the state offers more opportunities than local control for riches, patronage, and coercive power.

However, the inability to completely take over the state means that the hybrid actor also operates outside the state to maintain its capability, legitimacy, and power—even as it seeks certain inroads into the state apparatus. It develops parallel structures that can act as a check on the state, if certain state actors decide to check the hybrid actor's power. Operating outside the state is also crucial for the hybrid actor's role in the political economy of conflict. These armed groups benefit from patrolling their own checkpoints and taxing (or extorting) populations to generate revenue. These processes would be more complicated if the state interfered and enforced additional mechanisms of accountability. The gray area between state and nonstate, therefore, allows the hybrid actor to prosper.

Proxy or Ally? Relationships with External Patrons

Hybrid actors often are closely aligned with an external sponsor. In most cases, this external actor helped support the hybrid actor from its earliest days, providing resources, training, and opportunity to the group's leadership. The current framework for understanding these hybrid actors treats them as "proxies" for their patrons, which in the Middle East and North Africa are primarily Iran, the United States, Turkey, and the Arab states of the Gulf. However, analyses that treat hybrid actors simply as proxies deny them their agency; hybrid actors do have agency, and at times domestic political considerations force them to deviate from or reinterpret their patron's demands. In fact, many hybrid actors are more consumed with internal competition within their countries than with the demands of their external patron.[19]

For instance, Iran is widely regarded as the most successful implementer of the proxy model. From Hezbollah in Lebanon to paramilitary groups in Syria and Iraq (the PMU), the common narrative is that these groups must comply with Tehran's demands. However, as this report details in each case, hybrid actors at times stray from their patrons' priorities when their local legitimacy, capability, or power would be threatened. At other times, the hybrid actor will comply, particularly when its interests converge with those of its patron. In most cases, it is therefore best to understand the relationship between the hybrid actor and the patron as an alliance.[20] "Proxy-ness" exists on a spectrum, and the degree to which each hybrid actor is a proxy varies greatly. The hybrid actor is neither a puppet nor a wholly independent power. Crucially, it can shift back and forth over time—at times behaving like a proxy, at others like an autonomous state, and at still others like something in between.

Characteristics of Hybrid Actors

Hybrid actors are, at their core, armed bodies, and they come into being by having the capacity to provide security and services to their constituents. They provide security by employing fighters, creating security checkpoints in cities, and fighting armed insurgencies (such as that of the Islamic State). When a hybrid actor successfully uses such measures to fight off an insurgency that the state has failed to confront, the group gains a significant amount of power and legitimacy with its constituents. The state may even end up depending on it. In Lebanon, for example, many came to see Hezbollah as the only reliable defender of the nation. And for its members, Hezbollah has even become the protection from the state itself—part of the nation but above the rule of law. Other features of Hezbollah's provision of security are more general characteristics of hybrid actors: securitized zones, shared security agreements, no-entry zones, military training zones, permission of illegal trade for members and allies, no legal repercussions for crimes committed by members, and military engagement in neighboring countries.

Another characteristic of hybrid actors is their economic self-sufficiency, which allows them to survive—even at those times when they chose not to hew to their patrons' wishes. For instance, the PMU receives money from the state, but also engages in formal and informal economic activity (discussed in greater deal in the case studies below).[21] Similarly, Hezbollah members and supporters head municipalities in their areas of control, have multiple dealings with international aid and development organizations, control key ministries, and have representatives in parliament. But Hezbollah also has a parallel social service and economic network (both legal and illegal) that acts as a shadow economy and a source of power outside state control. With this mix of activities, hybrid actors are able to choose their proximity to the state while maintaining a flexible position: They insist on autonomy but do not openly refuse to pledge loyalty to the state. They participate in the political process but nonetheless have their own spaces where they enjoy a degree of sovereignty.

Hybrid actors also are able to provide basic services for their citizens, at times when the state fails to do so. For instance, the PMU in Iraq has taken over garbage contracts to clean the streets of Basra, in an effort to gain popularity. Beyond waste management operations, the PMU provides public services and infrastructure such as hospitals, clinics, schools, and roads; it also supports the families of "martyrs" who lost their lives in conflict against the PMU's opponents. These civic initiatives are inextricably connected to the PMU's military operations. Like a state, which provides security as well as services to the citizens that it governs, a hybrid actor views its mandate as encompassing the entire spectrum of human needs. Furthermore, the provision of social services enhances the hybrid's military capability. Service networks are embedded into the social fabric. For example, Hezbollah does not make a distinction between a Hezbollah fighter and a Hezbollah engineer—the individual may be employed as an engineer but fight in Hezbollah's forces on the weekend. Hezbollah is more than a security organization; it is a social, political, and economic network. Hybrid actors' provision of social services is also an efficient way to shore up constituents' commitment to their ideology, whether religious or otherwise.

To cement their power, hybrid actors rely on ideology. The most successful hybrid actors have a social mandate and a coherent, mobilizing ideology. But ideology is not the hybrid actor's distinguishing trait; other nonstate actors that lack the characteristics of hybridity still have social engineering projects and ideology.[22] Most commonly, hybrid actors instrumentalize ethnosectarian identity to build constituencies and gain support. For instance, the PMU recruited Shia fighters by invoking the image of the June 2014 Camp Speicher massacre, in which the Islamic State executed 1,566 Shia Iraqi Air Force recruits.[23] This ideological message appeared in speeches, posters, and other media. Hybrid actors tend to emphasize their ideology at times of heightened conflict. However, their commitment to ideology oscillates according to necessity, as does the character of the ideology. Hybrid actors often do not have one single governing ideology, but rather multiple intertwined grand narratives that can be highlighted at different junctures.

The rise of hybrid actors problematizes states' accountability and capacity. The hybrids evolved as a response to state failure, which is often the result of the long-term erosion of central power, competing power centers, and shared sovereignty. Hybrid actors have been able to fill a need that the state was responsible for providing but which it could not provide (or was not interested in providing). The mature hybrid actor, however, becomes an impediment to inclusive, equitable, and effective governance. It is immune from the state's wider burden to govern all its citizens. If the hybrid fails to adequately provide health care, security, or a sense of belonging, it is essentially off the hook—those are the state's responsibility, after all, and if the hybrid is able to furnish any degree of those goods it can be considered a bonus.

A stronger hybrid actor does, however, display a much greater level of legitimacy and recognition, as compared to earlier iterations that focused primarily on armed force and the wielding of brute power as a result. Hybrid actors retain flexibility linked to their use of force and violence; that need is not all-consuming, but all the same it is a lever for those seeking to incrementally influence the evolution of such groups. For outside actors, recognizing distinctive traits is essential for the crafting of coherent policy. Proper categorization and analysis can help lead to more appropriate and realistic policy choices.

II. Case Studies

The cases chosen for this report reflect a variety of nonstate activity, with some of the groups clearly functioning as durable hybrid actors. The examples of the Popular Mobilization Units (PMU) and Hezbollah offer a staggered view of how the phenomenon of hybridity has evolved over time and the linkages that exist between these related phenomena. The factors that have produced hybrids are separated by decades but largely have remained constant, though actor and sponsor capacities have only increased over time as expertise and opportunity have increased.

The report also includes cases of nonstate groups that appeared poised to become hybrids, or possessed some traits of hybridity, but did not fully translate those circumstances into sustainable hybridity. In the case of Syria's National Defence Forces (NDF), the group or some of its elements could have evolved in the direction of becoming a PMU-like, Iranian-backed parallel power as the Damascus government's authority diminished during the most testing periods of the Syrian war. In fact, however, the NDF remained attached to the state, and more firmly so as the government's military momentum increased. Amal, by contrast, represents a different model of evolution, that of voluntary transformation into traditional party politics. Amal is now fully invested in the Lebanese state and does not function as an armed group or militia.

In the case of the main Iraqi Kurdish parties, the KDP (Kurdistan Democratic Party) and the PUK (Patriotic Union of Kurdistan), these groups have achieved a unique hybrid status within both the autonomous Kurdish region (which some scholars identify as an unrecognized state) and the Iraqi state. Despite their links to the Kurdistan Regional Government (KRG) and Baghdad, the parties retain some of their flexibility beyond the limitations and institutions imposed by Iraq's various levels of governance. The Iraqi Sahwa, by contrast, sought to parlay its military advances into political power, but failed to do so as it lacked the ability to project power without the continued support of its outside patron and the outright hostility of the host state.

Finally, the phenomenon represented by the Islamic State is, in many ways, sui generis. The Islamic State clearly was not a hybrid actor, and it made no pretensions or efforts at achieving that kind of status. Armed with its ideology and transnational ambitions, the Islamic State sought to directly supplant and replace the state, and in so doing raised direct questions about statehood and stateness. As a result of its catastrophic impact on the region and its singular vision, the Islamic State merits discussion as a contrasting phenomenon to the hybrid actor model discussed in this report.

Some cases that have arisen within the geographic boundaries of this inquiry were not included in this report, but are worthy of further analysis using the model and criteria proposed here. The examples of the People's Protection Units (YPG) and Tahrir al-Sham, in particular, offer an opportunity to examine patterns of behavior arising with varied forms of outside state support. Further studies of hybridity ought to look at these and other actors, including in other MENA conflict zones and in other regions.

The Popular Mobilization Units of Iraq

The swift rise of the Islamic State, which conquered one-third of Iraq in the summer of 2014, mobilized tens of thousands of Iraqi men to defend their country. Rather than joining the retreating and collapsing Iraqi army or police, most of these men enlisted in paramilitary groups under the newly formed Popular Mobilization Units (PMU, or al-Hashd al-Sha'abi in Arabic). The Iraqi Shia cleric Grand Ayatollah Ali al-Sistani issued a religious decree (fatwa) calling on volunteers to rise up to fight the Salafi-jihadist organization.[24] Although Sistani's decree only mentioned the Iraqi state's armed forces, most volunteers chose to join the PMU. An umbrella organization of some fifty paramilitary groups with 110,000 fighters on paper (and closer to 80,000 active fighters on the ground), the PMU would become the main fighting force to defend Iraq from further Islamic State advances and to begin reclaiming territory in 2014 and 2015.[25] Although the Iraqi armed forces have since recovered, the PMU remains a powerful military force with an unparalleled ability to mobilize fighters, generate millions of dollars each month from both state salaries and illicit trade, and influence Iraqi politics at the national and local levels.

As a hybrid actor, the PMU's emergence is a consequence of the weakness of the Iraqi state, which was on the brink of collapse when a few thousand Islamic State fighters established the capital of their "caliphate" in Mosul, Iraq's second-largest city. Today, the PMU at times fights to defend the state and at other times competes with the state over legitimacy, capabilities, and power. As such, in definitive hybrid actor fashion, it has gained political influence inside the state *and* set up parallel state networks. Rather than placing the PMU under the Ministries of Defence or Interior—as the Iraqi constitution mandates for any armed force—Nouri al-Maliki (prime minister 2006–14) placed the PMU under the supervision of the prime minister's office, where it has remained ever since.[26] The PMU formally answers to the chairman of the prime minister's National Security Council (NSC), but its de facto leader is Jamal Jafaar Mohammed Ali Ebrahimi, popularly known by his nom de guerre, Abu Mahdi al-Muhandis, or simply Abu Mahdi.

Seven of the PMU's paramilitary groups had been operating in Iraq for several years before the group's formal creation in June 2014. These groups included the Badr Organization, Asa'ib Ahl al-Haq, Kata'eb Hezbollah, Kata'eb Sayyid al-Shuhada', Harakat Hezbollah al-Nujaba', Kata'eb al-Imam Ali, and Kata'eb Jund al-Imam. Additionally, the Peace Brigades (Saraya al-Salam), formed by Muqtada al-Sadr in June 2014, was in fact the remobilization of the notorious Mahdi Army, the major predominantly Shia armed group during the first civil war (2006–8).[27] Many of the other armed groups, such as Asa'ib Ahl al-Haq and al-Nujaba', were also remnants of the Mahdi Army. The Badr Organization was the oldest group, formed in Iran in 1982 as an Iraqi paramilitary group (then known as the Badr Brigades) to fight against Saddam Hussein during the 1980–88 Iran-Iraq war. After the U.S.-led invasion in 2003, Badr emerged as a dominant armed actor in Iraq. It eventually captured the Ministry of Interior and maintained an armed presence outside the state apparatus.

In the summer of 2014, the establishment of the PMU began a formalization process that brought in the existing paramilitary groups and invited many more groups to form. According to several PMU leaders, 2014 marked the beginnings of the second Iraqi republic, after the failure of the first republic (2003–14) in the wake of the Islamic State's announcement of a caliphate.

From 2014 to 2018, the PMU was not a monolithic group. Although the fight against the Islamic State united all of its members, the paramilitary groups within the PMU had different ideologies and ideas for their role with regard to the Iraqi state. The PMU was split according to the source of emulation ("taqlid") they subscribed to—between groups that primarily answered either to Iranian supreme leader Ali Khamenei, Sadr, or Sistani. The PMU's fighters could support more than one of these leaders, but this categorization serves as an important tool to understand the diverging ideologies within the umbrella organization.

At the start, the strongest groups within the PMU were those closely allied to Khamenei. These groups became the primary drivers of the PMU's state-building program, and as such they were the architects that transformed the PMU from merely an armed group to a hybrid actor. Beyond military capabilities, the groups allied closely to Iran developed (or maintained) political platforms, competed in the 2018 national elections, administered economic policies, and generated revenue. More recently, however, various PMU members have asserted their independence from Iran, sometimes actually condemning Tehran's interference in Iraqi affairs. This change underlines the degree to which the PMU is not a mere proxy for Iran. Instead, it is a fully hybrid entity, driven at least as much by local political concerns as foreign patronage.

The strength of the PMU has clear implications for policy and for the state. The PMU's state-like powers arose in part because of a vacuum left by the weak Iraqi state. Now, however, the PMU is nearly impossible to dislodge or to fully integrate into state institutions. Thus, the PMU has established itself as a fundamental limit on the state's ability to exercise its functions. Furthermore, the PMU has achieved legal status and secured funding from the state, while retaining its autonomy, entrenching its militias as competitors to the state's armed forces, and deepening the fragmentation of the monopoly of legitimate violence.

Relationship with the State

The 2003 invasion of Iraq not only dislodged the Ba'athist leadership from power, but also changed the structure of the Iraqi state, which had been built by British political officers in 1920. The Coalition Provisional Authority stripped the state of institutional legacies when it disbanded the Iraqi security sector and the top tiers of the civil service across government ministries, agencies, and affiliated institutions. This "de-Ba'athification" process, which sought to purge senior Ba'ath party members from public employment, weakened the state. For some armed actors, this policy presented an opportunity to gain power, while still keeping independent formations outside the state. It was the birth of the hybrid actor in Iraq.

Immediately after the invasion, the Badr Brigades moved from Iran to Iraq.[28] The group would become both part of the state and separate from the state. Its primary geographic location, in the initial years after the invasion, was along the eastern governorates bordering Iran, from Diyala to Kut (Wasit). When the Coalition Provisional

Authority issued an order to dissolve militias in 2004, the Badr Brigades moved around the law by rebranding itself as the Badr Organization and partly merging with the state. From 2005 to 2008, the
organization integrated some of its fighters into state bodies, primarily
into the Ministry of Interior. Many fighters joined the federal police,
which is housed within the ministry. As a result, Badr increasingly
took control of the ministry, installing its own minister, deputies,
and directors general. However, at the same time, Badr maintained a
separate armed wing outside the state. Thus, Badr became one of the
first hybrid actors to emerge. In 2014, with more than a decade of
experience operating inside and outside the state, Badr became the
largest paramilitary group of the PMU.

The Mahdi Army also emerged after the 2003 invasion. It initially resembled an insurgency or warlord, contesting the state and
refusing to work with it. Based on the legacy of Muqtada al-Sadr's
father, Mohammad al-Sadr—a popular Baghdad cleric assassinated
in 1999 for his defiance of Saddam Hussein—the Mahdi Army
quickly rose to prominence in 2003 and mobilized up to 60,000
fighters, making it the main armed group in Iraq at the time.[29] It
became notorious for major human rights violations and war crimes,
including brutal "death squads" and frequent raids, abductions, and
arbitrary killings in Sunni neighborhoods. It was deeply involved in
the sectarian war of 2006 and 2007. After the bombing of the Askari
Shrine in Samarra, one of the holiest sites in Shia Islam, Mahdi fighters initiated a wave of attacks against the Sunni population.[30]

In contrast to Badr, the Mahdi Army's insurgency made the
group a threat to the state. Sadr became associated with sectarian
rhetoric and anti-state activity. In the initial years after the 2003 invasion, the Shia Islamist parties, which had come from abroad, worked
with Sadr to keep the Shia house united. But eventually, as these Shia
Islamist groups gained control of the state, Sadr lost favor with them.
The Mahdi Army began as a militia led by local warlords loyal to Sadr
and opposing the regime, with several leaders ideologically opposed
to Sunni groups.

Maliki's first term (2006–10) was defined by a drive to strengthen the state and flush out insurgencies and anti-state armed groups, especially the Mahdi Army. In 2008, Maliki sensed an opportunity to bring down the Mahdi Army and directly fought Sadr in the Battle of Basra in 2008 (also known as Operation Charge of the Knights).[31] The Mahdi Army was subsequently disbanded. However, Sadr kept a small force underground.[32]

Maliki had little chance to bask in victory. In 2010, his State of Law Coalition lost the parliamentary election to Ayad Allawi's Iraqi National Movement (also known as the al-Iraqiya List), which was more secular and also included Sunni groups. To maintain the premiership, Maliki sought help from Iran as well as from paramilitary allies, including Badr and remnants of the Mahdi Army that had moved away from Muqtada al-Sadr. Maliki tested the limits of the law by working with these armed groups. He also set a new precedent by bringing them under the purview of the prime minister's office. These PMU armed groups thus become hybrid actors, working with the state but outside the constitution.

To court Badr—the primary hybrid actor at this point—Maliki made its leader, Hadi al-Amiri, his minister of transport. In his second term, which began in 2010, Maliki also relied on the existing pro-Iranian militias.[33] He worked with these groups to bring down potential challenges to his rule, including the 2011 protests in Sunni parts of Iraq—known as the Harak al-Sha'abi.[34] These paramilitary groups, which served as hybrid actors that worked with the state as well as outside the state, eventually formed the core nucleus of the PMU. Maliki brought them together as a way of providing an initial state cover to the mobilization of militias against the Islamic State—militias that many Iraqi commentators argued were illegal.[35]

Since the PMU's founding in 2014, Abu Mahdi, its de facto military head, has been preoccupied with legitimizing the PMU as a state institution while maintaining independence from the command structure of the central government.[36] The PMU leadership's desire to become a state actor is based on pursuit of both financial rewards and the legitimacy that comes with state recognition. From its inception, its leaders despised being referred to as militias; they claimed that they were fighting for the state in order to defend and recapture Iraqi territory from the Islamic State.[37] The key to Abu Mahdi's hybrid model, therefore, has been to become a state actor so far as it is financially and politically rewarding, but to maintain a line of independence from state accountability. This preoccupation reflects a concern with legitimacy and stateness that is common to many hybrid actors and often distinguishes them from warlords and classic proxies.

The rewards for becoming a state actor are clear. Financial gain is an obvious one. As an oil-rich rentier state, the Iraqi central government is a major source for revenue. Its annual budget, $111.8 billion in 2019, is one of the largest in the region.[38] As a PMU checkpoint commander put it: "You can make a lot of money from checkpoints. But if you control one ministry in the government, you can make ten times more."[39] Becoming a state actor also entails another layer of legitimacy that the PMU sorely needed after the main fight against the Islamic State ended, because of the constitutional prohibition of militias. Even Sistani's carefully worded fatwa, which PMU leaders used for recruitment, called on all Iraqi citizens to volunteer to join the armed forces rather than militias. According to various national polls, Iraqis in general reject the presence of nonstate militias and prefer state-recognized actors.[40] For all these reasons, the PMU's leadership perceived becoming a state actor as a top priority.

The PMU's relationship with Maliki allowed the group to claim that it was not a militia, but rather a state institution. In reality, the legal standing of the PMU was still in question, particularly following the abrupt end of Maliki's premiership. Maliki had built the alliances with the paramilitary groups, but his successor, Haider al-Abadi (prime minister 2014–18), was fundamentally opposed to the idea of the militias.[41] At varying points in his premiership, Abadi signaled his desire to integrate the paramilitary groups into the state armed forces.

Abadi presented a challenge to the PMU leadership, which felt the need to solidify its institutional presence during—and not after—the fight against the Islamic State. Abu Mahdi pushed for greater official recognition of his group by using the PMU's role in protecting the state as his bargaining chip. During the heavy part of the fight against the Islamic State, as the Ministry of Defence and Ministry of Interior struggled to recover, Abadi needed the PMU's help. But the PMU leadership was suspicious of Abadi's future intentions for their organization. They sought a greater legal standing, and their position was made stronger by their popularity, fighting prowess, and daily sacrifice of martyrs in the struggle to defend Iraq from the Islamic State. Abu Mahdi's capitalized on this popularity to publicly challenge Abadi with a letter, sent in October 2015, complaining that Baghdad was not paying the PMU as much as other fighters, and was thus jeopardizing the fight against the Islamic State.[42] Eventually, Abadi was forced to concede. In February 2016, he passed an executive order that stated that the PMU would "be an independent military formation and a part of the Iraqi armed forces, and attached to the general commander of the armed forces."[43] This wording was met Abu Mahdi's intentions of transforming the organization into a state-recognized force that nonetheless would be an "independent" military unit. In November of the same year, the Iraqi parliament passed a law that established the PMU as "an independent military formation as part of the Iraqi armed forces and linked to the Commander-in-Chief [the prime minister].[44]

With this law, the PMU leadership had cemented its status as a hybrid actor. It was part of the state but not under the constitutionally mandated armed forces. It had its own chain of command that did not go through the prime minister (it was only "linked" to him) but rather through Abu Mahdi. And with this law, Abu Mahdi also preempted future concerns for his organization about what could happen if changes in the executive branch reduced the PMU's influence or if a victory over the Islamic State led to renewed calls for demobilization.

The PMU as a Political Actor

Along with its military activities, the PMU has been a political actor. In the 2018 national elections, several major PMU groups ran together under the Fatah Alliance (or Conquest Alliance), headed by Badr Organization leader Hadi al-Amiri. Since Iraqi law strictly prohibits armed actors from running for office, the PMU groups changed their electoral names, repeating a practice they had used in earlier elections. Badr ran as the Badr Organization, Asa'ib Ahl al-Haq ran as al-Sadiqoun, Ansar Allah ran as the Honesty and Loyalty Movement, Sayyid al-Shuhada' ran as the Victorious Bloc (Muntasiroun), and the Khorasani Brigades ran as Vanguard (Tali'aa). Fatah finished second in the election, with forty-seven seats, losing to Muqtada al-Sadr's Sa'iroun coalition, which had fifty-two seats.[45] This election revealed the patronage strength of both the PMU and the Sadrist movement.

The leading groups within the PMU were not new to politics. Since 2003, many of these leaders had moved back and forth between the front lines and the government offices in Baghdad. As discussed above, for instance, Ameri was a minister from 2010 to 2014. In the 2014 election, Badr had won some twenty-two seats, and Sadiqoon had one seat. To lobby the government and participate in elections, the PMU has thus required a political wing. Although the political blocs have different names, the line between security and politics remains blurred. Abu Mahdi remains the driver of the PMU's influence over the government.

The PMU uses its power in parliament as a tool to lobby for friendlier policies and greater legal standing. Its strong political representation in the 2014–18 parliament, including its twenty-four seats and its allies in Maliki's State of Law Coalition and other members of parliament, helped the PMU's politicking efforts for the November 2016 law, which formally recognized it as a security organization. The PMU's even greater representation in the 2018–22 parliament has allowed Abu Mahdi to successfully lobby for a greater share in the national budget. In March 2019, the PMU scored a success when

parliament agreed for it to have pay parity with other security institutions. In effect, the parliamentary budget increased the PMU's own
budget by 54 percent. The PMU's allocation from the budget is now
nearly $2.2 billion (some 2.6 billion Iraqi dinar), which is allocated
to 122,000 fighters.

After the 2018 elections, the PMU's strong showing meant that
it played a major role in selecting the new prime minister and council
of ministers, along with Sadr's Sa'iroun. As such, the PMU's leadership was instrumental in the appointment of new prime minister
Adil Abdul-Mahdi. The main priority for the PMU leadership seems
to be to avoid a strong and adversarial prime minister. Compared
with Abadi, Al-Mehdi is in a weaker position as prime minister: he
lacks political party backing and owes his power, at least in part,
to the PMU. To further maintain influence, Abu Mahdi supported
the appointment of Mohammed al-Hashimi (known by his nom de
guerre, Abu Jihad) as the prime minister's chief of staff. Abu Jihad,
a strong PMU ally and close to Iran, helps oversee the PMU's relations toward the state. Abu Jihad has outlined his plans to tackle the
post-2003 state by removing officials—deputy ministers and directors general who are known in Iraq as part of the private grades and
wikala system. Under this system, since 2003, Iraqi political parties
have been sending appointees to staff government ministries and
agencies with an eye to gaining influence.[46]

The PMU has also sought influence over Iraqi governorates and
their councils, and state institutions. From predominantly Shia to
predominantly Sunni and mixed governorates, the PMU leadership
has focused these efforts in key governorates, including Diyala, Basra,
and more recently even Nineveh (Mosul). In several governorates,
the PMU has appointed its own candidates as governor—the high-
est position at that level.[47] Part of the PMU's interest in controlling
local governance is to pressure the central government. The PMU
can use its influence over local officials to lobby for its priorities in
Baghdad. In Basra, for example, the PMU convinced Governor Assad
al-Eidani to openly lobby against Abadi in a parliamentary session in

September 2018. Eidani criticized the prime minister for his failure to send sufficient and promised funds to Basra.[48] This lobbying ultimately ended Abadi's chances of reelection that year.[49] Further, focusing on the local level has allowed the PMU to develop local patronage networks that become important during elections. In Diyala, the PMU's strong patronage networks supported the Conquest Alliance to win the 2018 elections with 20 percent of the vote.[50]

Relationship with Constituents

From its inception and throughout the fight against the Islamic State, the PMU remained popular among constituents, particularly in predominantly Shia governorates. In a National Democratic Institute poll over the summer of 2015, 99 percent of Shia respondents claimed they supported the PMU.[51] Most residents recognized the sacrifices made by many of their own local volunteers fighting to liberate their cities in the north. They even referred to the group as the "Holy Mobilization Units" ("al-Hashd al-Muqadis"). Much of the PMU's popularity at the time stemmed from its ability to provide both security and services to its constituents. Its leaders showcased their ability to do so by using mainstream media outlets, social media, and other communications tools. The PMU website focuses on the group's provision of services.[52] The PMU sometimes provides security and other services in cooperation with the state, and at other times acts outside of it.

The end of the Islamic State's caliphate as a territory has led to questions about the PMU's continuing relevance as an autonomous hybrid security and services provider. Many Iraqis, including the PMU's own constituents, argue that the organization needs to fully transform into a state actor. In Basra, for instance, residents and civil society activists said that they had a general distaste for militias operating outside the Iraqi armed forces, including the PMU.[53] Although almost one-third of PMU fighters came from Basra, the 2018 protests also featured attacks on PMU member offices, including those of the Badr Organization.[54]

Facing calls to demobilize and integrate, Abu Mahdi has instead focused on maintaining hybridity. He has transformed the PMU from a wartime to a peacetime organization by carving out a space for it in the state. Part of this move includes addressing the concerns and demands from constituents by offering a vision for the PMU role as a security and services provider in a "post–Islamic State Iraq." As a hybrid actor, the PMU responds to the government's direct calls for assistance but also operates outside the government's command structure. However, in both cases, maintaining a popular base and constituency is important to the PMU leadership.

Whether during the war with the Islamic State or afterward, the provision of security has been a cornerstone of the PMU's relationship with its constituents. In the early years of the fight against the Islamic State, when the state's security apparatus was in a state of collapse, the PMU was the first on the front lines to defend the northern and western approaches to Baghdad, including areas such as Jurf al-Sakhar and Abu Ghraib, where the Islamic State was advancing. Eventually, the PMU had a free hand in liberating territories from the Islamic State outside of Baghdad. Its ability to defend Baghdad and other areas from the Islamic State, at a time when the Iraqi army and police were withdrawing, gave the PMU greater popular legitimacy.

Although the main fight against the Islamic State has ended, it remains a threat in certain governorates. In this context, Abu Mahdi's model for the PMU's relationship with the state has been to use the group as a sort of national guard, which will continue to fight the pockets of the Islamic State that still exist.[55] As such, the PMU commander works with local fighting groups, including Sunni, Shabak, Turkmen, Yazidi, and Christian PMU groups in northern Iraq.[56] The other main PMU groups help reinforce these local brigades. The continuing insecurity in certain pockets of the country allows the PMU to justify its strong military presence and operations in those areas.[57] The PMU also works to protect mosques and religious institutions, as well as religious pilgrims and festivals, such as Ashura.

Another part of Abu Mahdi's peacetime transformation of the PMU is to maintain the group as a crime-fighting organization. This move allows him to showcase its security provision capabilities while also cleaning up the image of the organization, which many Iraqis have begun criticizing for partaking in criminal activity, from oil and gas smuggling to racketeering and the drug trade. Previously, the urgency of the campaign against the Islamic State took precedence, and so the PMU could exist as a loose umbrella organization that housed a few criminal factions because its contribution to the war effort helped constituents overlook any corruption. But peacetime has brought new scrutiny, necessitating a cleanup. In August 2019, the PMU announced the arrest of Hamza al-Shammari, known as "Hamza Roulette" for his gambling empire. Shammari was close to Maliki and certain PMU groups such as Kata'eb al-Imam Ali.[58] As part of its communications campaign, the PMU showcased its shutdown of casinos, roulette, gambling mafias, drug dealers, and the sex trafficking markets in Baghdad and other parts of Iraq.[59] The PMU has also released news of its units capturing oil and gas smuggling fields in northern Iraq.[60]

The PMU's crime-fighting turn fits with Abu Mahdi's centralization and consolidation of power, turning the PMU into a sustainable hybrid actor. He can remove problematic groups and leaders under the banner of combating criminal activity.[61] Senior PMU leadership can also consolidate power and centralize its command structure, both jailing criminals (and internal enemies) and burnishing its image as capable police. This process began with the arrest of prominent paramilitary leader Aws al-Khafaji in February 2019.[62]

That said, the PMU's security provisions are not always in line with the state's command structure. For instance, according to a source inside the PMU, in September 2017 Prime Minister Abadi initially rejected Abu Mahdi's decision to take Kirkuk from the Kurdish peshmerga.[63] However, when Abadi realized that the PMU was already moving for Kirkuk, he quickly changed his position to maintain leadership over the security campaign. In this case, then, the

PMU dictated a security agenda that was later accepted by the state's command structure.

The PMU's communication campaigns have also highlighted its ability to provide essential services to citizens—services that the state has failed to deliver.[64] Over the past few years, protesters in southern and central Iraq have demanded better services from their government—especially better electricity and water—as well as employment. The 2018 Basra protests were in part a response to water contamination in the city that sickened many residents and placed the governorate on the brink of a cholera outbreak.[65] Protesters went to the streets to demand change. The PMU engineering units, in response, began building pipes to deliver clean water.[66] Many Iraqis also are concerned about the electricity supply, which becomes particularly problematic in the summer months when the country's scorching heat requires power to generate fans and air conditioners. In the summer of 2019, the PMU announced that different state actors were calling for PMU help in providing electricity—help the PMU was happy to say it would provide.[67]

More generally, the PMU has positioned itself as an emergency response unit that can quickly provide services after disasters, and as a quasi development agency that can help war-battered areas rebuild.[68] Following flooding in the summer of 2018, the PMU's engineering unit publicized its efforts to rebuild tens of kilometers of potholes and roads between Basra and Maysan.[69] PMU engineering units are also active in providing services in many parts of Diyala governorate where the state is absent and unable to. In February 2019, after more flooding, the PMU repaired a bridge in Diyala within hours of its collapse.[70] The PMU has also stressed the importance of rebuilding factories and reviving Basra governorate's local industrial production, including its famous date industry.[71] It has begun rebuilding schools, public squares, swimming pools, sports clubs, and youth and student clubs.[72] The PMU also provides other essential goods and services, including medicines.

Despite its emphasis on providing security and services, the PMU is not always able to completely satisfy many Iraqis. And when it faces protests that threaten its power and legitimacy, the PMU at times responds with force. Civil society activists throughout Iraq argue that the PMU has ramped up its repression of dissent. According to a humanitarian worker who operates a nationwide telephone helpline, a majority of the calls that the worker's organization receives are from victims who report violations by PMU fighters or leaders.[73]

The PMU's policy of repression became evident during the 2018 protests in Basra, in which citizens demonstrated against the continued lack of basic public services. On September 8–9, 2018, according to multiple sources inside the city, twenty-three protesters were shot and killed, and many more wounded. Several activists and analysts claimed that the perpetrators of the killing were supported by the PMU. Since then, activists in Basra have argued that the PMU is responsible for quieting the demonstrations by killing protesters. Indeed, after these incidents, protesters stopped going to the streets. Since then, Basrawis who refuse to protest say that the main reason they abstain is the memory of violence from September 2018.[74]

Relationship with Patron (Iran)

The PMU has never operated as a monolithic group. Instead, it is an umbrella organization of groups with varying ideological standpoints and relations with the main patron, Iran. Some groups, such as Kata'eb Hezbollah, Harakat Hezbollah al-Nujaba', or Saraya al-Difa'a al-Sha'abi, take direct orders from the elite Quds Force of the IRGC, led by Qasem Soleimani. As a Nujaba' fighter put it, "we are ready to fight the United States in Syria, for example, but we cannot move without the green light from Iran."[75] These groups would be considered proxies, insofar as they serve Iranian interests in Iraq. However, these groups are paramilitary organizations that either support or challenge the state, depending on the circumstances. For instance, when Prime Minister Adil Abdul-Mahdi issued a decree in July 2019 to integrate the PMU into the government, some PMU member groups, including

Kata'eb Hezbollah, rejected the decision. As such, these groups are hybrid in that they are state-recognized actors that are not accountable to the state and, at the same time, operate as nonstate actors.

The main PMU groups—whether they are closest to Khamenei, Sistani, or Sadr—lie on different parts of the proxy spectrum. In a hallmark trait of hybrid actors that perform state-like functions, these groups must sometimes decrease the degree to which they act as proxies for sponsors. These actors often seek to gain local power, popularity, and legitimacy from their constituents, which often proves incompatible with complete fealty to a sponsor.

Over the years, polling data suggests that Iraqis have become wary of Iran—the main patron of the PMU. Iraqi pollster Munqith al-Dagher has found that "the percentage of Iraqi Shiites who have favorable attitudes toward Iran decreased from 88 percent in 2015 to 47 percent in the fall of 2018. During the same period, those who have unfavorable attitudes toward Iran increased from 6 percent to 51 percent."[76] Thus, a public perception that the PMU acts as a mere proxy for Iran hurts the group's standing with constituents. PMU leaders undoubtedly are aware of this concern, and in recent years have moved away from sectarian or Shia-centric discourse and toward a nationalist Iraqi discourse.[77] Part of this shift is in response to growing resentment among Iraqi Shia against Iran. In Basra, this resentment was clear in the summer of 2018 when protesters burned down the Iranian consulate. Any PMU leader looking to become a political actor—and a hybrid actor—must therefore account for these changing trends in Iraqi public opinion.

Ever since the invasion of 2003, Shia armed leaders who transition to politics have tended to distance themselves from Iran as part of their transition. Sadr and his Mahdi Army, for instance, were at one point aligned with Iran in the fight against the occupying U.S. forces, but over the years moved away from Iran and turned into an Iraqi nationalist actor against Iran. This switch became evident when Sadr returned to Iraq (from exile in Iran) in 2011. Sadr's rhetoric had dramatically shifted. He now openly condemned Iran for its destabilizing role in Iraq. In some ways, Sadr's defiant independence from foreign sponsors has been a lynchpin of his appeal. Today, Sadr continues to stake out an anti-Iran position as part of his bid to represent the Iraqi street and protest movement, which has been known to chant, "Iran, out, out."[78]

Even among the pro-Khamenei PMU members, there are those like the Badr Organization's Ameri who have had to make local compromises—and maintain the appearance of greater independence from Iran—in pursuit of national office in Iraq. Ameri was once considered a direct Iranian proxy for his role fighting with Iran against Iraq during the war between the two countries in the 1980s. But Ameri, too, began shifting his rhetoric during the fight against the Islamic State as he became a national figure and sought further institutional power in Iraq. He similarly employed more Iraqi nationalism and opened up to relations with the West. Ameri also began deviating from Iran's orders. For instance, one month after the 2018 national election, he decided to form an alliance with Sadr's anti-Iranian Sa'iroun coalition, in his pursuit to become a greater Iraqi leader. This move upset Iran, which then began working with Asa'ib Ahl al-Haq leader Qais Khazali to undermine Ameri and upset the alliance, which ultimately fell apart. Any leader of a hybrid armed group who seeks a greater role in Iraqi politics has at some point had to consider more local (and national) factors and as a result move away from direct control as a proxy of Iran.[79]

In short, many PMU members rely on a foreign patron when necessary or convenient—in other words, when doing so enables them to receive funds, weapons, training, and access to equipment—but will move away from the foreign patron when the group becomes more self-sustaining and politically minded.

Hezbollah of Lebanon

Lebanon's Hezbollah is often held up as the exemplar of nonstate actors or proxies. It has played a decisive role in Lebanon since its establishment in 1982, and it has evolved into a savvy and influential regional force. Iran's long-term investment in Hezbollah appears to have paid handsome dividends. Hezbollah has developed a durable, loyal following in Lebanon, and a military capability without parallel in the region. Hezbollah's intelligence, expeditionary, and command-and-control capabilities match those of many state militaries with far greater resources. The tight collaboration between Iran's leadership and Hezbollah is frequently cited as a model of what a clever patron can produce.[80] But no other hybrid actor in the region has achieved Hezbollah's stature. Iran has failed to replicate its Hezbollah success elsewhere, although it has identified best practices based on Hezbollah's development as a powerful hybrid actor.[81]

A close study of Hezbollah's trajectory suggests that a unique set of circumstances led to its development. Hezbollah originated in equal measure from indigenous local forces and foreign intervention by its patron—since its foundation, it has been hybrid. Hezbollah's enduring power as a hybrid actor also reflects Lebanon's special status as a weak state whose authority and legitimacy are distributed among a large number of warlords and religious and identity groups, none of which is strong enough to dominate all the others. Lebanon's fragile equilibrium has not been replicated in other countries, despite the echoes of Lebanon's approach to sectarian power-sharing in Iraq's apportionment system. The fragmentation and lack of capacity inside the Lebanese state have contributed to Hezbollah's endurance as a hybrid actor. Competitors of Hezbollah have, for the most part, been uninterested in strengthening state institutions as a way of constraining or balancing Hezbollah, because any such move would also limit their own room for maneuver.

History and Founding

Hezbollah was founded in 1982 (although the group kept its existence secret until 1985), at a time when the newly established Islamic Republic of Iran had a policy of trying to actively export its theocratic revolution to the rest of the Islamic world. Iranian state agents were working overtly and covertly with groups and individual activists whom it considered potential allies of the Islamic Republic's activist agenda. In the early 1980s, Lebanon was a particularly inviting recruiting ground. Since 1975, the country had been in the throes of a stop-and-go civil war. It hosted a vast array of militant groups that had developed pipelines for financing, weapons supply, and training. Every state that had an active foreign policy in the Middle East was involved in the Lebanon conflict. Every armed group had at least one foreign sponsor state. Furthermore, Lebanon's historically marginalized Shia community had achieved demographic, economic, and political heft such that its members expected—at a minimum—parity with the country's Sunnis and other confessional communities. Finally, Lebanon held a special symbolism for Iran's Shia clergy. When Persia adopted Shia Islam as its official religion in the sixteenth century, clerics were brought from Jabal Amel, in southern Lebanon, to teach the new faith. Commercial and educational ties continued to connect the Shia population centers of Jabal Amel to Persia and then Iran until the present day.[82]

Musa al-Sadr, the cleric most credited with leading the Shia political awakening and propelling Lebanese Shia to organize political parties and militias, was himself born in Iran but made his name in Lebanon. He established the Supreme Islamic Shia Council in Lebanon in 1969, and the Amal Movement in the 1970s, both of which still play important roles in Lebanese Shia life today. Sadr disappeared in Libya in 1978, and is believed to have been killed by the regime of Muammar Qaddafi. By the early 1980s, the politicized and militant Shia activist class that Sadr helped catalyze had fractured. Some young Shia fighters and clerical students fought on behalf of the Palestinian factions that were dominant in the Lebanese Civil War in the early 1980s. Some stayed with Amal, a Shia political force that was not committed to Ayatollah Ruholla Khomeini's theocratic principle of the Rule of the Jurisprudent ("Wilayat al-Faqih" in Arabic, rendered "Velayat-e-Faqih" in Persian, and sometimes translated as the "Guardianship of the Jurist"). Some established a theocratic offshoot in Lebanon, which they called Islamic Amal. Some left Lebanon altogether to study in the seminaries of Qom or Najaf, or to organize underground with groups like the Shia Iraqi Islamic Dawa Party.[83]

In 1982, Iranian Revolutionary Guard Corps (IRGC) soldiers assembled a group of willing militants in Baalbek, Lebanon for training. This group became the nucleus of Hezbollah. The group has never fully accounted for its operations between 1982, when it was founded, and 1985, when it publicized its existence under the name Hezbollah (meaning "Party of God," a phrase from the Quran). It eventually took responsibility for some attacks, like the suicide bombing of an Israeli base in Tyre in 1983, while it has encouraged ambiguity and never taken direct responsibility for attacks in Beirut the same year, on the U.S. Embassy and American and French barracks.

Throughout the 1980s, Hezbollah evolved militarily and politically. Syria supported the Amal movement while Iran backed Hezbollah, and at the time Syria was significantly stronger in Lebanon. Hezbollah earned the unremitting enmity of the United States and of some European governments because it kidnapped and sometimes killed Western civilians. Although other groups pioneered the use of suicide bombings in Lebanon, Hezbollah emerged as the most frequent utilizer of the tactic. Hostage taking, suicide bombing, and an early focus on soft civilian targets prompted Western governments to label Hezbollah a terrorist group, a designation that has followed Hezbollah even as it matured into a quasi-governmental hybrid actor.

Throughout the 1980s and early 1990s, Hezbollah established itself as an increasingly effective military force and as the most persistent opponent of Israel's nearly two-decade occupation of Lebanese territory. After occupying Beirut in 1982, Israeli forces had retreated to the southern portion of Lebanon by 1986. Most Lebanese parties and militias rhetorically opposed the continuing Israeli occupation, with the exception of some Christian factions that were directly allied with Israel. But it was Hezbollah, virtually alone, that continued to fight Israel. In 1992, Hezbollah made a decision to enter electoral politics, standing candidates for parliament. In 2000,

Israel withdrew from almost all the territory it occupied in Lebanon, as a direct result of Hezbollah's military campaign. By that time, Hezbollah itself had largely forsworn the tactics that had prompted many Western governments to designate it a terrorist group. Nevertheless, it still resorted to assassinations of Lebanese rivals and occasional terrorist attacks against civilian Israeli targets.

Syria took de facto control of Lebanese politics and much of its territory in the settlement that ended the civil war in 1990. In 2005, some Lebanese revolted against Syria's heavy-handed control, after the assassination of former prime minister Rafik Hariri, in a plot most likely linked to Hezbollah and the Syrian government. A Hezbollah raid into Israeli territory in 2006 sparked a month-long war in which Israel destroyed much of Lebanon's infrastructure. The war killed approximately 1,300 people in Lebanon and 165 Israelis. Hezbollah emerged from that period stronger and more autonomous than ever, with renewed political legitimacy and public support. The weakening of Syria's position greatly increased Hezbollah's room for maneuver. Since its founding, the group had relied on Iranian funding and weapons supplies, but it needed Syria's logistical backing in order to train, travel, and receive money and weapons shipments. After Syria was forced out of Lebanon in 2005, the balance subtly shifted in Hezbollah's favor—now Syria's regime needed Hezbollah in order to exert influence over Lebanon.

That balance shifted further in Hezbollah's favor in 2011, when the Arab uprisings spread to Syria. Popular anger against Bashar al-Assad's regime flared in Syria. Hezbollah initially tried to stay above the fray, and its secretary general, Hassan Nasrallah, offered to mediate between disaffected Syrians and the regime. But the Assad regime violently suppressed peaceful protests, and by 2012 faced an armed revolt. Hezbollah and Iran, the regime's only reliable supporters at that stage, agreed to extend military and financial support. At the time, it was not clear even to supporters of the Assad regime whether it was possible to preserve the family's rule or even the existing state institutions. Instructively, another hybrid actor, the Palestinian faction Hamas, broke with the Assad regime after enjoying its support and protection for decades.[84]

For Hezbollah, the uprisings created a dilemma. The group had developed legitimacy and popularity in Lebanon and across the entire Middle East and North Africa through its support for the "dispossessed" against rapacious rulers. Despite its Shia religious identity and support for Rule of the Jurisprudent, Hezbollah claimed a non-sectarian and trans-sectarian identity as a militant actor fighting for the oppressed, regardless of their identity, against "imperialist aggressors" like the United States and Israel. And the initial revolt in Syria was neither sectarian nor religious in nature. The Syrian regime is dominated by members of the Alawite sect and relatives of the Assad family, but it is not a sectarian regime as such. Syria's population is majority Sunni, but Syrian Sunnis are anything but a monolithic bloc; they include secular and religious people, supporters of the regime as well as leaders of the revolt. In general, Hezbollah sided rhetorically with the poorly governed people of the Arab world against the authoritarian dictators who ruled them. Hezbollah claimed to have created a counterexample, by providing better services to its constituents, avoiding corruption, and subscribing to an ideology that connected the organization to its community. Hezbollah intrinsically opposed power for power's sake. All these positions might at times have reflected the party's rhetoric more than its practice and motivations, but they nevertheless formed Hezbollah's core political appeal. Based on these factors, Hezbollah might have been expected to support the Syrian uprisings, as it did almost all the public uprisings against Arab dictators. But Syria, where the dictator was a key ally, was an exception. Hezbollah was not sure whether the Syrian government could survive, but considered its support critical enough that it was willing to publicly yoke itself to the Assad regime.[85]

Hezbollah supplied critical military support to the Syrian regime, including thousands of its own infantry soldiers. Hezbollah fighters, or Hezbollah military planners working closely with IRGC officers, led many of the sieges and urban military campaigns in Syria. It created a new network of bases for supply and training on Syrian territory, and in a departure from practice before 2011, Hezbollah and Iranian forces had autonomy from Syrian oversight in areas under their control. Reports and public statements suggest that Iran and Hezbollah shared a common strategic and tactical vision for the Syrian war, but that their plans often encountered resistance from Syrian officials, who could veto the proposals of their backers despite their weak position.

By 2018, the military conflict in Syria was limited to a few zones in the east, northeast, and the northern governorate of Idlib. Syria's principal allies—Hezbollah, Iran, and Russia—reduced the tempo of their military operations. Hezbollah has withdrawn some of its troops from Syria and has renewed its rhetorical emphasis on the conflict with Israel, which has remained more or less frozen along the lines of the settlement of the 2006 war. Hezbollah also speaks regularly of its support for the Houthi government in Yemen.

Inside Lebanon, Hezbollah's position is as dominant as it has ever been. Its principal Christian ally, the Free Patriotic Movement, controls the Lebanese presidency and the cabinet. Hezbollah and its allies can steer government policy, although Lebanon's consensus system empowers the minority to hold veto power over cabinet decisions, so even the dominant group cannot override a minority or opposition veto. Militarily, Hezbollah is stronger than the Lebanese Armed Forces, and in any case the leadership of the Lebanese state's military coordinates with Hezbollah and in no way opposes it.[86]

However, this strategic, political, and military concentration of power has come at a cost. Hezbollah has had to direct a great share of its resources to the war in Syria, and has had to recruit at least twice as many fighters to maintain its militias. The organization has gained a great deal of experience in urban combat, and in coordinating with other militias, but it has been forced to neglect its vast network of social services. Hezbollah's leadership found it more difficult to persuade its supporters that the war against fellow Arab Muslims in Syria was part of its core mission, although this argument gained traction once the Islamic State and al-Qaeda offshoots gained strength and Hezbollah could portray the uprising in Syria as part of a transnational "takfiri" jihadist plot to destroy pluralism in general and the Shia community in particular.[87]

Relationship with Constituents

Hezbollah's strength is built on the deep trust and credibility it has cultivated with its constituents. By the 1990s, Hezbollah had evolved and adapted its message and organizational identity, styling itself as a protector of dispossessed Lebanese Shia, of Lebanon against Israel, and of Arab independence against foreign intervention. Hezbollah did an effective job crafting a compelling ideology, delivering services to its supporters, and providing a security umbrella through its highly committed military forces. The organization thus was able to win profound loyalty, despite the obvious internal contradictions in its message. Hezbollah's leaders openly bragged about the support they received from Iran, while deriding their rivals for receiving support from other outside powers. The thrust of their appeal rests on three axes of constituency building: identity, security, and services.

Ideology and Identity

The first axis is Hezbollah's "resistance ideology," which includes elements of religion, governance, and ambition for state building.[88] Hezbollah has thrived with state backing from Iran, which supplies the ideological core through the Rule of the Jurisprudent. Along with Zionism, the ideology of resistance has been one of the most successful political, social, and state-building projects in the modern Middle East, as measured by hard power accrued, followers recruited, and ability to steer culture and geopolitical events. Resistance ideology often has evolved in explicit opposition to Israeli policy, while at the same time borrowing mobilization and state-building techniques from Israel and the Zionist movement.

Hezbollah's ideology has bound its followers into a coherent community and also governs its relationship with its state patron. Hezbollah's Shia-inflected ideology of resistance enables it to mobilize its core supporters—devoted believers from the Lebanese Shia religious community—around a project of building a faith-based society. The same ideology appeals to people who identify as Shia but are not so pious. Finally, with a slight shift in emphasis from religion to resistance, Hezbollah can appeal to a wider and looser population of constituents who either are not Shia or, in some cases, are not religious at all.

In a 2016 speech thanking international supporters of "the resistance," Hassan Nasrallah emphasized constituency as a central ingredient in Hezbollah's ability to thrive in the face of better-armed and better-funded adversaries:

> One of the main elements of strength of any resistance is its popular embrace and environment—the people who support this resistance and back it and offer it their children, and hold the funerals of its martyrs with pride, and show tolerance when they are wounded and when their houses are destroyed, and when their fortunes are being blazed down. They tolerate displacement and do not harm the resistance with a word. They [prefer to] support it with all their strength and back it to be able to proceed.[89]

In a different speech later that year—a decade after the 2006 war—Nasrallah reminded his followers that there was always an enemy to rally around and that, while other groups slackened in their willingness to engage in perpetual war, Hezbollah preferred to fight as a mode of day-to-day existence: "The future of Lebanon is the Resistance, the future of Palestine is the Resistance, and the future of Syria is the Resistance," he said. "The future of the region is the future of our peoples and our nation and its dignity, pride, and sovereignty."[90] In Hezbollah's formula, economic benefits are a boon but not a necessity for securing ongoing support.

The resistance axis has prioritized social mobilization since its early years, investing in public art, public spectacles, documentary films, and cultural programming, along with news and music, as vectors of ideology formation.[91] Al-Manar television and Al-Nour radio offer strictly controlled official news and programming, including children's shows and religious education.[92] Private channels, websites, and social media streams burnish the ecosystem of Hezbollah content.[93]

Security

Within Hezbollah's area of control inside Lebanon, the group has a monopoly on force. Lebanon's other security forces, which notionally are national, do not set foot in Hezbollah areas unless under special dispensation and with Hezbollah's permission. Hezbollah has its own intelligence, police, and military forces, in charge of internal and external security. Compared to other communities in Lebanon and the wider region, Hezbollah has managed to deliver a higher level of security than any of its peer competitors. Internally, Hezbollah areas are comparatively safe. Organized crime does not compete with Hezbollah, and mainly exists in Hezbollah areas with the party's acquiescence—in some cases because organized crime is controlled by powerful clans in the Beqaa Valley or in districts of South Beirut where Hezbollah must tacitly ally with crime bosses in order to consolidate geographical control.

Externally, Hezbollah's military forces fight effectively under the organization's chain of command.[94] They have proven an effective deterrent against Israel, as evinced by the relative calm along the Israel–Lebanon border since the 2006 war. (Hezbollah sometimes refers to this mutual deterrence as a "balance of terror".) Hezbollah infantry and officers have fought in Yemen, Iraq, and Syria, developing a reputation as disciplined fighters and effective field commanders.

For Hezbollah's constituents inside Lebanon, the party's security apparatus has brought dividends. Members of Hezbollah's community enjoy a curtain of protection that makes them less susceptible to violence or extortion from members of rival communities. It also entitles them to a greater share of government patronage or immunity from government rules.[95] Hezbollah's control of border crossings, for example, has created a vibrant trade in illegally imported goods, which are sold in Hezbollah areas at a lower price than in other parts of Lebanon because the import duties were never paid.[96]

Services

Since the party's founding, Hezbollah has emulated an Iranian approach of providing services to constituents through foundations that nominally are not under the party's control but in fact are directly controlled by Hezbollah members loyal to the party leadership, or by clerics close to the Iranian leadership. These service-providing foundations blend with other Shia charitable foundations that are *not* under Hezbollah's de facto control, like the Al-Mabarrat Association, established by the late Lebanese cleric Grand Ayatollah Mohammad Hussein Fadlallah.

Hezbollah members can expect a full, high-quality social safety net that enables them to live at a middle-class level and provide their children with a college education. The party runs a network of schools, clinics, hospitals, youth scouting associations (the Mahdi Scouts), and foundations that provide ongoing financial support to the spouses and children of Hezbollah members who are killed in combat. It also supports committees that promote women's education. Casual supporters enjoy Hezbollah's security umbrella and access to some of the party's services, such as clinics, but not the total financial support given to members. Needless to say, Hezbollah links all the services that it provides to its ideological mandate. The web of services and ideology helps maintain loyalty among constituents and buttresses Hezbollah's ability to mobilize support. When the party's finances have come under strain because of Iranian cash flow limitations, Hezbollah officials openly discuss their budget constraints. Their comparative frankness in the Lebanese context, and the consistency with which Hezbollah has delivered services to constituents since its founding, enhance the party's credibility.

Assessing Constituent Dedication

Hezbollah's constituency has been the group's cornerstone. In the group's first decade, Hezbollah experimented with coercion and conversion as it tried to foist an austere model of religious governance on the Shia of Lebanon. That approach backfired, limiting Hezbollah's appeal to a small group of ultrareligious Shia who believed in theocratic governance. By the 1990s, Hezbollah had switched to a persuasion model. Without abandoning its core religious beliefs and devotion to the principle of the Rule of the Jurisprudent, Hezbollah put "resistance" at the forefront of its ideological program. The organization's fighters proved dedicated to the military struggle against Israel and, over time, were increasingly effective. This combination of mobilizing, organizing, and delivering on key promises won a devoted following. Hezbollah's supporters and members trust the organization and have shown themselves willing to volunteer in service, whether military or civilian, at the group's behest. Critically, Hezbollah's followers have been willing to trust the organization's leadership through acknowledged mistakes, like triggering the 2006 war, or through transitional periods such as 2011–13 when Hezbollah was entering the Syrian war without the full buy-in of its Lebanese supporters.

It is certain that Hezbollah also employs coercion. The group is believed to have detained, tortured, and killed people whom it considers to be working against the organization's interests, and it suppresses any political challengers within the Shia community. Its only historical rival within the Shia community, the Amal movement, was tamed by the 1990s, and now occupies a role as political interlocutor for Hezbollah with movements and states that refuse to talk to Hezbollah directly. Amal has a patronage network and a significant political network, but its political power is amplified by the support it receives from Hezbollah and by Amal's role as a conduit to Hezbollah. Unlike other authoritarian movements, Hezbollah tolerates a zone of public criticism within its community, just as it must accept criticism from rivals because of the pluralistic nature of Lebanon's political system. The result is that Hezbollah prefers to persuade its supporters rather than compel them; usually, it deploys violence only against outsiders who challenge the group directly or constituents who are accused of working as spies.

The loyalty of Hezbollah's constituents has given the party more political flexibility than its peers. In Lebanese elections, Hezbollah performs more reliably than any other party. It does not lose public support from its core constituents even when members are connected to violence, corruption, or deceit. For example, the murder of former prime minister Rafik Hariri threw Lebanon into turmoil and for a time threatened Hezbollah's political project. Evidence from international investigators convincingly showed that Hezbollah, working with the Assad regime in Syria, conducted the assassination. Yet Hezbollah members have been willing to believe Hezbollah's unconvincing denials because they trust the group to provide a compelling identity and ideology, safety, and services.

Another and perhaps more important indicator of constituent loyalty is the support that Hezbollah is able to rally for its military ventures. According to the group's own statements, it has at least doubled the size of its fighting forces since entering the war in Syria (though it does not disclose an actual number of fighters). Hezbollah has been able to fill its ranks despite the high risk of frontline deployments in Syria and a steady stream of well-publicized deaths and casualties—analysts estimate that at least 2,000 Hezbollah fighters have died in Syria. Hassan Nasrallah frequently thanks the party's supporters for sticking with it during the "lean times" of the Syria campaign, when the party had to redirect resources away from the social safety net in Lebanon and toward the military campaign across Lebanon's eastern and northern border.

Relationship with the State (Lebanon)

In a quintessential hybrid actor balancing act, Hezbollah has cultivated a track record of operating within the state to acquire assets for patronage; coopting the state in order to steer its power and resources; and remaining at arm's length from the state so that it can function as a private entity and disruptive critic, taking no actual responsibility for state policy. This fluid relationship gives Hezbollah a form of political impunity, at least with its constituents: it can claim that all the state's failings are the fault of other Lebanese movements and coalitions. At the same time, Hezbollah can supplement the direct support that it receives from Iran with huge direct and in-kind subsidies from the Lebanese state: free electricity, public sector jobs for supporters, and direct support or complicity from state agencies that are supposed to restrict Hezbollah activity.

Hezbollah carefully positions itself as a legal and legitimate entity. Every time a new government is formed, Hezbollah insists that the ministerial statement refer to "the army, the people, and the resistance." Hezbollah also insists that it is willing in theory to merge its fighters into the national military—if only the national military were willing to act as a deterrent against Israel. These positions are more than just rhetorical gyrations; they reflect Hezbollah's bedrock desire to be understood as a legal and legitimate part of Lebanon's state and society, even as it stands just far enough away from the machinery of state so that it can avoid responsibility for governance failures.

The nature of Hezbollah's relationship with the Lebanese state is exceptional in the region, although there are parallels in Iraq, where a host of hybrid actors have reached maturity alongside the official state-building project. In the case of Lebanon, the state was in shambles at the close of the civil war in 1990. Different warlords and militias held sway in their limited fiefs. Almost all the competing groups defined themselves solely by sectarian identity. Only Hezbollah and its eventual partner, the Christian Maronite Free Patriotic Movement party, published platforms with nationalist, rhetorically inclusive, state-building projects as part of their political agenda.[97] Hezbollah was able to build up its operations and relationship with the state even as the state itself was being reconstituted in the 1990s, after the conflict ended. Helpfully, from Hezbollah's point of view, the state fell under Syrian tutelage, while Hezbollah itself was working closely with the regime of Hafez al-Assad in Syria. In some cases, the Syrians found it useful to exert direct control over activities in Lebanon; in others, they relied on loyal local partners, including Hezbollah. Until the Syrian withdrawal in 2005, Hezbollah intentionally maintained a low profile within the state, relying on Syria to steer state resources and protection to Hezbollah. Once the Syrians left,

Hezbollah pushed for a greater share of power in state institutions, and its allies worked more actively to secure Hezbollah's interests. It first secured a plurality and then a majority of the cabinet ministers for its alliance. Its parliamentary delegation took a more forward role in political debates. And beginning with the 2006 war, when Hezbollah's economic needs dramatically expanded as the group sought to rebuild areas devastated by the war, Hezbollah began to partake more visibly in the looting of Lebanese state resources through patronage and corruption.

Lebanon's idiosyncratic political system provides built-in constraints on Hezbollah's rise. Top jobs in the government are dispensed on a sectarian basis through an unwritten understanding that has governed Lebanese politics since independence in 1943. A Maronite Christian serves as president, a Sunni Muslim as prime minister, a Shia Muslim as speaker of parliament, and so on, with sectarian quotas down the line for other key positions, including army chief of staff and central bank governor. Hezbollah has intentionally kept out of this high-profile quota apportionment and has publicly criticized the practice.[98] In this manner, it enjoys the political dividends of criticizing a corrupt system and calling for its replacement with a nonsectarian democracy, while at the same time taking benefits by placing allies in key positions. After the 2018 parliamentary elections, for example, Hezbollah won just 13 seats, in keeping with the historic size of its parliamentary delegation, but its coalition controlled a commanding total of 72 of the 128 total seats.[99] The speaker, Nabih Berri, comes from the Amal movement, but almost never makes a move that counters Hezbollah's interests.[100]

In rare cases when state institutions threaten Hezbollah's interests, Hezbollah has not shied away from violence. In 2008, a simmering political standoff broke into violence when a Hezbollah rival tried to end Hezbollah's control of the Beirut airport. In a similar vein, a string of unsolved assassinations hampered the work of an independent tribunal investigating the Hariri murder—the investigation that uncovered compelling evidence of Hezbollah complicity. The

Lebanese government today is dominated by Hezbollah allies. So is the military. Minor fiefdoms, such as the Internal Security Forces, a sort of high-level national police entity, are loyal to rival parties but have only limited power.

Relationship with Patron (Iran)

The partnership between Tehran and Hezbollah anchors the "resistance axis." It is a coalition of affinity as well as interests. An analysis of Hezbollah as an Iranian proxy misses the normative and ideological dimensions of the partnership. The IRGC actively created Hezbollah out of preexisting indigenous Lebanese organizations.[101] The result is a like-minded, adaptive organization cut from the same cloth as its parent. Hezbollah officially claims the leader of Iran as its religious reference. There is no daylight between Hezbollah and Iran, yet the relationship is not one of subservience. Hezbollah manages its own affairs domestically, and it operates with autonomy (though always in concert) on matters of importance to Iran.

Iran remains Hezbollah's only patron and appears to be responsible for the group's entire budget. In the years after the 2006 war, Iran flooded Hezbollah with cash to rebuild war-shattered areas. But the war in Syria has monopolized most of the Iranian support for Hezbollah, which has, in turn, been constrained by the sanctions and U.S.-led pressure campaign against Iran. Nonetheless, the policies of Iran and Hezbollah have been virtually indistinguishable. There is no instance where Hezbollah visibly departed from Iran's goals in the region or in Lebanon, and Hezbollah's leaders have been unstinting and public in their declarations of fealty and gratitude to Iran. In almost every speech, Nasrallah thanks Iran for its support and credits the Islamic Republic with building a "resistance axis" across the region that is strong enough to counter the power of the United States, Israel, Saudi Arabia, and their allies. Nasrallah describes any prospective attack against Iran as an attack against all of Iran's partners. In a typical example of his speech, in a recent speech on International Quds Day—a pro-Palestinian, anti-Israel holiday created by Khomeini in

1979—Nasrallah spent almost the entire speech praising Iran. "Iran is a real state, a promising and rising state. It is progressing at the forefront of this axis. Well, this is our axis. These are very great elements of strength. They are unprecedented." Later on, he added: "Any war on Iran would mean the whole region [would] be set ablaze."[102]

At the same time that Nasrallah and other Hezbollah leaders habitually thank Iran, Iran carefully gives its Lebanese partner room to maneuver and, if it so desires, to distance itself from its sponsors—actions that suggest a relationship of trust between Tehran and Hezbollah. A recent example came during a state visit by Iran's foreign minister, Mohammad Javad Zarif, to Lebanon. Nasrallah thanked Iran for supporting "Lebanon, Palestine, and the resistance movements against both Zionism and takfiri extremism . . . despite the conspiracies and pressure Iran has been subjected to as a result. This assistance has led to victories in many arenas and battlefields."[103] Zarif, in turn, held a press conference with the Lebanese foreign minister, and said that Iran would be willing to support all of Lebanon's state institutions, not just "the resistance," if only the Lebanese military were willing to accept help from Iran. (The Lebanese Armed Forces takes support from the United States and maintains at least a nominal distance from Hezbollah and Iran.) "We don't want to embarrass anyone in Lebanon through the cooperation with the Islamic Republic," Zarif said.[104]

Iran and Hezbollah have an ideological and strategic confluence that makes their partnership particularly effective. Were Hezbollah to part ways from Iran ideologically—a change that would be hard to imagine given the organization's roots and history—Iran could withhold funds and weapons and Hezbollah's power would drop precipitously. Hezbollah has tremendous credibility with its constituents and tremendous power within the Lebanese system, but this power relies on Iranian resources that cannot be replaced by another source. Iran's financing to Hezbollah has fluctuated over time, but not as a function of a shift in commitment. After the 2006 war, for example, Iran flooded reconstruction funds into Lebanon. The reverse has been true since the Trump administration has intensified pressure on

Iran and suffocated Iran's economy; Hezbollah has seen a reduction in its budget without experiencing a loss of political clout. "The sanctions and the terror lists are a form of war . . . we should deal with them as if they are a war," Nasrallah said in a speech in March 2019, in which he solicited donations from supporters. "Their actions will not be able to make us poor, hungry or isolated. Those that support us will continue in their support—be they countries, people or our people and the people of resistance in Lebanon."[105]

Hezbollah's position has shifted along a spectrum with respect to Iranian control. At the beginning it operated as a type of pure proxy, but in its current maturity it often operates with state-like functions and as a sort of subsidiary peer. During the 1980s, in its revolutionary phase, Hezbollah sought to extend an Iranian-style theocratic culture to the Shia communities under its control. Such moves proved unpopular, and Hezbollah ultimately opted for a much more restrained approach than Iran's, promoting Islamic piety as a gradual grassroots process of social change rather than a top-down revolution. Hezbollah's leadership, and Nasrallah in particular, provide their own Arab, Shia analysis of political imperatives and strategic goals. In Arab contexts such as Iraq, Yemen, and Syria, Hezbollah provides an Arab face for Iranian machinations. There is some evidence that Hezbollah goes further, providing its own proposals and assessments, and shaping Iranian policy. Lebanese journalist Ali Hashem, who for years has been based in Iran, has written extensively about Iran's consultations with Hezbollah, and argues that Nasrallah's thinking helped drive Iran's decisions about how to handle Syria.[106] Hezbollah military officers reportedly work as trainers in Syria, Iraq, and Yemen, consolidating a long-term foothold for both Hezbollah and Iran.[107]

The National Defence Forces of Syria

The National Defence Forces (Quwat al-Difa'a al-Watani; NDF), a network of loyalist militias, was created in 2012–13 as an official, state-backed paramilitary force in support of the Syrian Arab Army

(SAA) and of Syrian president Bashar al-Assad's government. At its peak it included tens of thousands of armed men, some of whom functioned as frontline infantry soldiers while others were deployed in rear areas as a sort of home guard.

The NDF is an unusual case in that it evolved from both state and nonstate roots, top-down as well as bottom-up, by regularizing fragmented loyalist factions within a state-linked but Iranian-backed institutional umbrella. It developed some of the attributes of a hybrid group and could have evolved in a direction similar to Iraq's PMU, becoming a semiautonomous security force under Iranian influence. But the Syrian central state acted early on to rein in such tendencies and keep the NDF within its chain of command. The NDF case illustrates the centrality of state authority (or its absence) in shaping a conflict environment that can constrain or enable the growth of hybrids.

Rather than a monolithic organization, the NDF is an agglomeration of lightly armed, semi-integrated local armed groups, tasked with the defense of their home areas and with contributing troops to SAA-led offensives as needed. The group is officially sanctioned by the Syrian government and appears to be linked, in legal terms and possibly also on top leadership levels, to the Ministry of Defense.[108] However, the NDF is not considered part of the SAA under Syrian law, and like many other progovernment militias the government instead refers to it as part of the military's auxiliary forces ("al-quwat al-radifa").

Despite its important role in the Syrian war, little has been written about the NDF, and the history of its creation remains shrouded in secrecy. Fieldwork in Syria has not been possible, and the account in this report has been pieced together from a variety of sources, including the NDF's prolific online propaganda, various progovernment and opposition accounts, and interviews with researchers and others who have insight into Syrian militia operations.

History and Founding

The NDF's establishment appears to have been motivated by the Syrian government's desire to control, empower, and restructure the many irregular militias that by 2012 had emerged in loyalist communities and on the initiative of individual officials. It also was intended to function as a channel for external support from Iran, and the rapid growth of the NDF in 2012–13 reflected efforts of the Islamic Revolutionary Guard Corps (IRGC) and Hezbollah to build a militia movement in support of Bashar al-Assad's government. These two functions of the NDF—a government-imposed restructuring of militias and a conduit for Iranian support—appear inextricably entwined, and each is key to understanding its role.

The NDF's organization can be divided into three tiers: national, governorate, and local. NDF integration with the Syrian state and regime appears to be high on the national level, but some of the local militias at the bottom end of the structure bear little resemblance to organized military units and may be better understood as nonstate actors incorporated into a state-structured hybrid framework.

Very little is known about the NDF's organization at the national level, but it appears to take the form of one or more institutions that coordinate activities within the movement and control salary pay-ments. Other support functions, such as ammunition supplies, also may be handled at this level. The central structure seems likely to be affiliated with either the Ministry of Defense, the Republican Guard (one of the government's most trusted elite units in Damascus), or the presidential administration, and it includes a body known as the NDF's General Secretariat. Although Iranian Revolutionary Guard Corps (IRGC) support helped construct the group, the NDF project appears to have been managed from the Syrian end by Brig. Gen. Bassam al-Hassan, an influential Syrian Republican Guard officer from the Homs region who has served as Assad's adviser for strategic affairs. Hassan's nephew, Saqr al-Rustom, was selected to form the first NDF governorate-level center in Homs, and later took office in the General Secretariat.

The most visible level of leadership within the NDF is not the General Secretariat or other national institutions, but rather the governorate-level centers. Their geographic distribution follows

Syria's standard administrative division into sixteen governorates, with one exception: the Damascus and Damascus Countryside governorates appear to have been combined into a single NDF center. Each center is led by a regional commander who (unlike the secretive national-level leadership) tends to be well known in his area. Typically, this person will either be a retired senior SAA officer or a civilian militia leader with personal links to the Assad family or other relevant power brokers, such as Rustom.

The governorate-level centers are charged with the administration and leadership of local NDF units, which typically are composed of men (or in rare cases, women) from a single city, city district, or village. These groups vary wildly in terms of size, equipment, composition, and professionalism. They originally grew out of the popular committees ("al-lijan al-sha'abiyah"), a form of proto-militia movements created in 2011 and 2012, which the opposition referred to as "Shabiha."[109] According to a defector from Syrian military intelligence, the first committees relied mostly on unemployed Alawite village youth and street toughs ("qabadays"), who were organized by village officials and elders under loose security agency oversight. In 2011 and 2012, his military intelligence unit was stationed in Kassab, near the Turkish border:

> Our station in Kassab was manned by eight guys only, but we were responsible for several villages. Our boss . . . was responsible for organizing security in the villages around us. He made contact with the various villages, with the mukhtar [village head] or someone else who could get it done, and told them to form popular committees to manage their own security. What we did was to put up three roadblocks in each village. There would be one at the entrance, one in the middle of the village, and one at the exit on the other side. Then the committees would be in constant contact with him. They could call the station any hour of the day to coordinate. Their job was to search

cars and to look for bombs and guns and things of that sort. They didn't have a right to go around arresting people. They had no special rights. If they found something suspicious or if there was a problem, they would call us and someone would come down from the station to solve the problem.[110]

In Homs as on the coast, according to Carnegie Middle East Center researcher Kheder Khaddour, early pro-Assad militancy relied on young, poor, unemployed, and relatively uneducated Alawite men from working-class neighborhoods or nearby villages. "Initially armed with sticks," he writes, volunteers manned strategically placed checkpoints in residential neighborhoods. They were tasked with controlling vehicle entry to the area and reporting to the secret police, or mukhabarat, "any individual that they found suspicious." The mukhabarat "would also organize young volunteers from the committees to take part in pro-government demonstrations. . . . The more educated members tended to be the sons of army or secret service officers and it was to them that fell the task of organizing the Shabiha groups."[111]

The Assad family and most of the top brass of the SAA and the security agencies are Alawites, a small minority in Syria, and although the Syrian government is formally secular and enjoys some level of cross-sectarian support, it is very disproportionately favored by religious minorities.[112] Alawites consequently appear to have made up the overwhelming majority of the popular committees on the coast and in all religiously mixed areas with a significant Alawite population, such as Homs. The committees would otherwise "mirror the ethnic, religious and class composition of the neighbourhoods they protect," in the words of a UN Human Rights Council investigatory panel.[113] In Aleppo, for example, members of a Sunni clan, the Berris, came to the aid of the government in 2011.[114] In al-Qusayr, members of a Christian family with links to the security apparatus, the Kasouhas, took it upon themselves to run checkpoints on behalf of the government.[115] In Idlib, local officers relied on a small set of

Sunni businessmen and Ba'athist families to organize popular committees that would beat up demonstrators and help the police track down opposition sympathizers.[116]

As the conflict grew more intense and violent in the summer of 2011, many of these groups started to evolve into armed militias, clashing with rebels and taking over responsibilities from the overstretched SAA. This development brought its own set of problems, as poorly disciplined committee members began to impose themselves on their local communities and attack rivals with impunity. Nestled inside a broader political conflict between supporters and opponents of the Syrian government, vicious spirals of local and sectarian violence began to emerge, often pitting Alawite popular committees against Sunni opposition fighters who referred to themselves as members of the Free Syrian Army (FSA), a vaguely defined name or brand that many different armed groups appropriated.

As political scientist Stathis Kalyvas notes, the phenomenon of local militias engaging in "predatory" violence is common to civil wars across the world. "Their reputation for atrocity is well established," he writes in *The Logic of Violence in Civil War*. "They may cause an escalation in violence because they use their power to fight personal or local conflicts."[117] Syria was no exception, as many of the worst instances of communal violence in in the 2011–12 period have been linked to vengeful popular committees. The Independent International Commission of Inquiry on the Syrian Arab Republic, a United Nations–mandated investigative panel, noted reports that popular committees had engaged in "mass killings" with "sectarian overtones."[118] For example, popular committee militants from nearby Alawite and Shia villages apparently played a central role in the May 2012 massacre of civilians in Houla, a rebel-held Sunni enclave near Homs.[119] The government refused to acknowledge or prosecute any such abuses, and the SAA often was complicit in them. Still, at least some senior leaders appear to have been concerned by the chaotic growth of unstructured local militias. Already in April 2011, the Homs Governorate police chief felt compelled to order citizens to stop forming popular committees and instead call the police in case of disturbances, apparently without much effect.[120]

It was this diverse, fragmented, and hard-to-manage landscape of hyperlocal militias that began to be restructured with IRGC support in 2012. By mid-2012, a first wing of what would become the NDF had taken shape in Homs, and the program then spread across the country in late 2012 and early to mid-2013. "There are a lot of these young guys, and it was necessary to bring some organization to the popular committees," a retired officer and leader in the Homs branch of the NDF told the pro-Damascus media outlet *Al Mayadeen* in 2013. "In Homs, wise people came and managed to discipline these people. It was necessary to have a wise leadership, and God blessed us with it in Homs. They managed to organize the guys and called them the National Defence Forces."[121]

NDF leaders used existing popular committees as a recruitment pool or simply swallowed them whole into the new NDF movement. Recruits were given light arms, salaries, and two weeks or a month of military drills; some were sent to Iran for specialized training.[122] Most importantly, they were incorporated into the NDF structure by being placed under the command of one of the governorate-level centers, which in turn linked back to the central node in Damascus. In practice, however, even after years of ostensible integration and streamlining, many local NDF units retained their local-militia characteristics and their original commitment to neighborhood or village. This enduring localism and internal fragmentation continues to shape NDF operations, limiting the state's ability to mold and direct the movement. At the same time, the loose nature of the structure also seems to prevent the NDF from taking on a more coherent corporate identity and developing collective political ambitions.

Relationship with Constituents

It is difficult to identify a distinct popular constituency for the NDF as a whole. Like other Syrian progovernment militias, it seems to have neither the ambition nor the capability to administer territory or populations—rather, it fights to roll back existing state institutions—and its members operate in separate governorate-level and local contexts. Although the NDF overall is lopsidedly Alawite and it is strongest on the coast and in the Homs region, it contains militias from a variety of political, ethnic, sectarian, or tribal backgrounds. NDF commanders are unlikely to view themselves as collectively representing any coherent national-level interest group, except the loyalist cause in general, and perhaps the interests of their fellow militia fighters in particular.

There is no evidence of an NDF political project either inside or outside Syria's existing institutional structure. For example, the NDF does not appear to have established political fronts or media mouthpieces, in contrast to what one would expect if the group were seeking influence as an organized entity. There seems to be no NDF newspaper, television channel, radio station, or even a website; its central messaging tool remains a simple Facebook page, which uploads NDF videos, information about battles, and pro-Assad propaganda.[123] Nor does the NDF appear to propagate a distinct ideology, in contrast to doctrinaire factions like the Syrian Social Nationalist Party (SSNP). The group's online propaganda reveals only the standard tropes of loyalist militancy—nationalism, militarism, and the glorification of Assad and his family—complemented by praise for the NDF itself and for its commanders.

As a collective, then, the NDF does not appear to support any particular constituency in Syria, beyond the loyalist cause generally and the welfare of militia members and veterans. However, many NDF leaders are heavily invested in local politics and commerce, and have developed followings in their home areas. Community members who feel that the NDF has saved them from chaos, Sunni Islamist rule, or massacres may view the militia leaders as heroes, but their relationship to host communities is not always straightforwardly protective or representative. To the contrary, many local NDF groups appear to be heavily involved in organized crime and smuggling, and they are notoriously ill-disciplined. Alawite pro-Assad militants in Homs not only preyed on Sunni neighborhoods for loot and money, but also forced well-off Alawites to "donate" to their war effort.[124] "After this crisis, there will be a 1,000 more crises—the militia leaders," a Syrian official told *Time* in 2013. "Two years ago, they went from nobody to somebody with guns and power. How can we tell these shabiha to go back to being a nobody again?"[125]

Having grown wealthy and powerful in their local context, NDF-linked figures are likely to try to use their local power base as a springboard toward positions of influence in the national economy or in the state's political and military institutions, whether individually or in interest-based networks. The past few years have in fact seen several examples of NDF-connected individuals rising within Syria's existing institutional order. For instance, many individuals with connections to militias have sought entry to municipal and governorate assemblies and the national parliament. Elections in Syria are unfree and at best semicompetitive, but nonetheless serve a purpose as a vehicle for the institutional cooptation and platforming of powerful individuals. Wealthy businessmen and tribal sheikhs commonly seek to advance their personal status by either joining the ruling Ba'ath Party or running for office as independents, typically by negotiating for a spot on candidate lists controlled by regime insiders.[126] During the war, militia leaders copied this behavior. For example, the 2018 municipal elections brought an NDF-affiliated candidate into the executive office of the Raqqa Governorate Council.[127] On a higher rung of the political ladder, Fadel Wardeh, an NDF leader in Salamiyah, near Hama, was elected to parliament in 2016 on a Ba'athist ticket and acceded to the party's Central Committee two years later.[128]

Businessmen with links to militias also play a part in Syrian business, and many commanders enjoy "extravagant lifestyles thanks to their side gigs as war profiteers," in the words of journalist Nour Samaha.[129] Some NDF leaders have used their money to start companies, whether as a side activity or to transform themselves into legitimate businessmen. For example, the head of the Quneitra NDF center, Khaled Abaza, co-founded Al-Fajr Guard and Protection Services, a security company.[130] In 2017, Rustom (the former NDF

Homs leader and General Secretariat official) and his uncle Hassan (the NDF's original central organizer) reportedly established a company called Damas Real Estate Development and Investment LLC.[131] By positioning themselves for a postwar reconstruction phase, they seem well placed not merely to profit but also to cater to the needs of militiamen, their families, and other potential constituents.

A particularly interesting project with links to the NDF is the Martyr Foundation, a humanitarian charity established in 2013. Saqr al-Rustom heads its board of trustees, and the executive director is a man named Nael al-Rustom; there is some evidence that the two are brothers.[132] Based in Saqr al-Rustom's hometown and stronghold, Homs, the foundation has branch offices in several other governorates, including Damascus, Tartous, Latakia, Aleppo, Hama, and Suwayda. In April 2014, the Martyr Foundation entered into a partnership with the Syrian Ministry of Social Affairs and Labor, to implement programs overseen by the ministry.[133] According to a website that is now defunct, the purpose of the foundation is to

> engage in social and charitable activities intended to defend the culture of martyrdom, to commemorate the efforts of the martyrs, to compile statistics of their exploits, and to keep their memory alive; in addition to caring for the general situation of their families and to compensate them, to the extent possible, in relation to the greatness of the sacrifices that the martyrs have offered and to the suffering encountered by their families after their martyrdom; in addition to caring for the wounded and following-up on their injuries until the healing process has been completed.[134]

The Martyr Foundation presents itself as a nonpartisan "youth project," and insists that it does not favor any particular faction of loyalist fighters, but it has specifically run projects to support wounded NDF fighters.[135] Its connection to the NDF seems to be well understood outside the group: in 2013, the Martyr Foundation's executive director at the time, Ahed al-Sukkari, had to begin an interview by refuting allegations that the foundation exists solely to aid NDF members and their families.[136]

"Though not exclusively for NDF veterans, [the Martyr Foundation] plays an important role in providing them services," writes Khaddour, who reports that it "builds hospitals, arranges funeral services and burials, plans leisure activities for children at schools, and provides material support to the families of members of the NDF."[137] Organizing hospital care for injured NDF members may be of particular importance to the group, since NDF members have reportedly (as nonenlisted personnel) been forced to pay for treatment at SAA-run military hospitals.[138] Khaddour concludes that the Martyr Foundation works on several levels apart from the purely humanitarian one—it raises the morale of NDF fighters, helps sustain and consolidate the loyalist community, and binds members closer to the group's leadership:

> Members of the [Martyr Foundation] and the NDF come from similar backgrounds; they are civilian, not military, and they come from the same local community. There is a tight linkage between members of the association and the NDF because fighters come from the same region, and often sect, as the local members of the association. The same family will often be involved in both activities— sending fighters to the NDF and supporting or being supported by the association. The presence of this association creates a general feeling of security inside the society for these fighters. It assures them that they are protected and that there is another civilian party that will support them and their families in the event of their injury or death.[139]

In October 2016, the head of the Martyr Foundation's Damascus branch, Rashad Ali, told an interviewer that the group was supporting a total of 22,645 families across Syria, with most beneficiaries in Tartous (9,116), Homs (5,968), and Latakia (4,187).[140]

It is not clear whether the Martyr Foundation has received Iranian support, but it appears to have been able to tap into several other funding streams: "Part of the funding is from international institutions like UNICEF or UNRWA [the UN organization that serves Palestinian refugees], and there is also self-funding through the clinics that will in some cases receive citizens for a low fee," Ali reportedly said. "There are also donors among the civil and economic actors and contributions from the members of the board of trustees."[141] According to Human Rights Watch, the Syrian Ministry of Foreign Affairs and Expatriates has placed the Martyr Foundation on a list of approved partners for the United Nations in Syria, from which UN and nongovernmental organization aid programs are obliged to select national implementing partners.[142]

Relationship with the State (Syria)

In eight years of war, Syria has witnessed a proliferation of armed factions, including on the side of the SAA. The central government has, in effect, outsourced military tasks to irregular militias, many of which are supported and controlled by specific security agencies, regime-linked businessmen, or even foreign nations. The scholars Antonio Giustozzi and Reinoud Leenders have characterized the diversity of the loyalist armed apparatus as evidence of a "heterarchical" system. "The Syrian regime's use of militias reduced the 'stateness' of authoritarian governance; yet it did not bring about the state decay, failure or collapse so often associated with the outsourcing of violence," they write. "State power came to be served, rather, by a heterarchical order, wherein state and nonstate coercive actors proliferated side by side and complemented each other."[143]

One may argue against the description of Syria's loyalist militias as nonstate actors, given that "state" activities may be broadly understood to include both routine institutional actions and private, state-sanctioned initiatives on the government's behalf. In fact, as we will see below, although many militias originally emerged through the mobilization of ordinary civilians and are structured unlike conventional military forces, they are significantly shaped by and linked to the state.

The Syrian government appears to have been aware that arming grassroots supporters and giving the IRGC access to local militias could create an ultimately uncontrollable Frankenstein's monster, but appears to have acted strategically to preempt such a development. "They have experience, if you go back to the sixties," said Khaddour, who points to the SAA's 1976–2005 operations in Lebanon and to now-defunct Ba'athist militias such as the Popular Army ("al-Jaysh al-Sha'abi"). The Popular Army "was created in the sixties after the Ba'ath Party takeover, and it was the same [as today's militias]. They have their own officers and they recruit people by themselves, but in the end they're under the army umbrella and that is what allows them to survive."[144]

In the case of the NDF, Damascus has sought to ensure loyalty and cohesion by working with and empowering trusted leaders; by keeping militias dependent on state and military institutions; by offering privileges to ordinary fighters; and more generally, by keeping militias embedded in the Assad regime's institutional, social, economic, and political order. As a result, the NDF appears to have remained consistently loyal to the Syrian government and reliant on its institutional support, which has prevented or disincentivized the development of hybrid attributes such as constituent governance and service provision, ideological distinctiveness, and logistical and practical self-sufficiency.

The primary lever of state control over the NDF is its leadership. The original organizers of the NDF appear to have been senior members in the Republican Guard. The man overseeing the project reportedly was Hassan, an Assad adviser. The process of building the NDF's governorate-level centers—its main nodes of control—also appears to have involved many retired SAA officers, several of whom played leading roles in the movement. Generally, these officers have held the ranks of colonel ("aqid") or brigadier-general ("amid"), although at least one major ("ra'id") appears to have led the Suwayda center.[145]

The regime's heavy reliance on ex-military personnel may simply have been a function of how its internal networks are constructed, or of retired officers' prominence within the popular committee militias that formed before the NDF was founded. But it also brought practical advantages. "Former officers are an effective means of ensuring the reenlistment of badly needed military manpower and expertise on the regime side, while at the same time acting as ambassadors of the regime in local communities," writes Khaddour. "Militia recruitment centers are local bodies with recruits often having close personal connections to the officers in charge. This dramatically increases the effectiveness of background security checks on new recruits and helps ensure the loyalty of those who are enrolled."[146]

Not all NDF leaders have a military background. Some of the most powerful provincial NDF chiefs were civilians with close personal links to senior regime figures. The best-known examples are Rustom and Hilal al-Assad, the president's cousin, who led the Latakia NDF from 2012 until his death in 2014.[147] Personal contacts with the ruling family also appear to have led to the appointment of Fadi Saqr as head of the powerful NDF branch in Damascus: Saqr was an obscure provincial director of the General Consumption Establishment, which oversees food and fuel distribution and pricing, but he also reportedly was a former bodyguard of Bassel al-Assad, the president's late elder brother, and a friend of Maj. Gen. Maher al-Assad, the president's younger brother. Similar mechanisms operated at the governorate level, outside the president's inner circle. For example, a Druze hotel owner and businessman named Rashid Salloum served as NDF leader in Suwayda governorate from 2012 to 2017, reportedly because of his connections with Brig. Gen. Wafiq Nasser, the governorate's head of military intelligence.[148]

In some cases, entrepreneurial militia upstarts took over NDF branches that initially had been led by officers. For example, the Aleppo NDF was first set up in early 2013 under the leadership of Col. Hassan Khashir, whose small band of fighters worked out of Khanaser to clear the Aleppo-Hama road. Khashir was killed in August 2013, which seems to have led to a rebooting of the Aleppo NDF. In late 2014, leadership had passed to Sami Oubri, an Aleppo car dealer and amusement park owner who had, since 2012, transformed himself into one of the city's leading militia paymasters. He retained the position until 2017.[149]

Many if not all of the loyalist figures selected to lead an NDF branch had begun to organize militias on the regime's behalf before the group's creation, reflecting their own strong interest in defending the prevailing order. The Quneitra wing of the NDF offers an illuminating example of how pro-regime provincial elites mobilized their personal networks to fight for Assad's government in 2011, how this helped sustain their relevance to the regime core, and how support from Damascus and Tehran through the NDF has continued to reinforce their dominance on the local level.

In 2012, an NDF center was established in the Quneitra governorate, which encompasses the Israeli-occupied Golan Heights and nearby areas. It later evolved into an NDF-affiliated militia known as the Golan Regiment (Fawj al-Jolan). Its members were Sunni Muslims, and some were in fact rebels who had been drawn back into loyalist ranks.[150] For several reasons, the Quneitra NDF might have seemed like a weak link in Assad's chain of militias: it was a relatively small group that faced great risks, including Israeli attacks; its members were Sunnis from a peripheral area without strong links to the regime and (at least in theory) had the option of switching allegiance to the rebels; and Iran's strong interest in the Golan Heights might mean that it would seek to build influence there at the Syrian government's expense. In fact, however, the Quneitra NDF appears to have remained as loyal to Damascus as any other NDF branch. Some clues as to why can be found by looking at its leadership.

The first and thus far only leader of the Quneitra NDF center was Khaled Abaza, a dentist from a prominent Circassian family with impeccable loyalist credentials and considerable influence in the region.[151] His father, Brig. Gen. Walid Abaza, was a powerful Hafez al-Assad–era security officer who had helped repress the Muslim Brotherhood uprising in Hama in the 1980s and had ended his intelligence career as second-in-command of the Political Security

Directorate. Now in his sixties, the elder Abaza still wielded great influence in his home region as head of the Syrian Ba'ath Party's Quneitra branch and as a member of the party's Central Committee.[152] The entire family seems to have joined the war effort: Walid Abaza came out of retirement to assist the government, first in Hama in 2011 and then in Quneitra, and his sons Khaled and Anzour took up arms against the rebels in their home region, presumably using support channeled to them by their father. Anzour was killed in 2012, and his mother, Jeansit Qazan, then emerged as a public figure by creating an association called Mother of the Martyr (Umm al-Shahid).[153] She was elected to parliament as an independent representative of Quneitra in 2016. When Walid Abaza fell ill and finally passed away in 2017, his surviving son Khaled inherited the office of Quneitra Ba'ath Party chairman, and since then has held both political (Ba'ath) and military (NDF) power in the Golan region.[154]

In other words, even though the Quneitra wing of the NDF was nurtured by Iranian support and relied on non-regime sources of manpower, such as defecting rebels, it remained tightly linked to trusted elites and Assad-controlled institutions: the Abaza family and the Ba'ath Party. At least in its leadership, then, the Quneitra NDF represented less a new and unfamiliar "Iranian" militia whose loyalty to Damascus had to be tested, than a weaponization of the regime's own prewar networks. This appears to have been the rule across Syria, rather than the exception.

Militias are also bound to Assad's government by an enduring structural dependence on state and military institutions, which provide their members with salaries, security clearances and permits, health care, and economic support. Indeed, despite an onset of institutional rot in government-held Syria, especially around its militia-infested fringes, everyday life for most of the population—which includes NDF members and their families—continues to be regulated by the politico-bureaucratic authority of the central state. And although the SAA has been hollowed out by the war, it remains in control of military logistics and specialized functions, including air support, heavy weapons, and ammunition supplies. "For stockpiles of arms, vehicles and basic food provisions the NDF have been fully reliant on supply centres within the regular army structure," write Leenders and Giustozzi.[155]

NDF-SAA coordination reportedly is facilitated by the embedding of military liaisons within the militias, without whom they could not function legally or practically in Assad-held Syria. "The army is not what creates the militias, but it structurally allows these militias to exist," Khaddour explained.[156] By way of example, he pointed to what amounts to a basic necessity for any paramilitary recruitment program: training facilities.

> The army is the hub or the base where all the militias can get training. It might not even be [Syrian] army training—it might be Iranian or Hezbollah or now also Russian training—but you must be in a base. You need space, simply. You can't train in a city. You must be outside, somewhere in the countryside. The Syrian military institution is the second biggest land owner after the Awqaf, the religious endowments. Most of these lands outside cities—the military sectors in Homs, Hama, in the south—are officially owned by the army.[157]

Institutional links to the state may weaken over time, especially if the state itself grows weaker and becomes less able to reward loyalty or punish disobedience. To some extent, this has already happened. For example, inflation has diminished the value of salaries paid in Syrian pounds, which makes militias depend more on alternative sources of income: smuggling, checkpoint taxation, looting, and support from private businessmen or foreign patrons. Already in 2012–13, militias in Homs were taking in protection money from Alawite businessmen and allowed fighters to keep a percentage of the profits from looted property in Sunni neighborhoods as a complement to their salaries.[158]

In that context, initiatives like the Martyr Foundation may serve to enmesh NDF members in parallel systems of semiprivate institutions. In turn, it is conceivable that the NDF could take on state-like functions and increase its autonomy from Assad's government, but such a transformation would require a considerable weakening of the existing order. Unless the Syrian government were to backslide into more serious structural decay, private parallel networks under loyalist control are more likely to be complementary to the state's own efforts. Indeed, as long as Assad remains in power and the Martyr Foundation remains under the control of solidly pro-Assad elites, its activities seem more likely to *increase* the connectedness of individual NDF fighters to the regime.

On the official and legal levels, too, the Syrian government has sought to incentivize voluntary recruitment and bind fighters and their families closer to the state.[159] For example, in December 2014, Assad decreed that 50 percent of all public sector vacancies would from then on be allotted to family members of fallen soldiers, including "civilian martyrs . . . working under the orders of the Syrian Arab Army."[160] In 2018, Assad decreed tax breaks for wounded soldiers wishing to buy locally assembled cars, and offered write-offs for loans of up to 1 million Syrian pounds to disabled former soldiers or militiamen, and families of deceased loyalist fighters. In 2019, local administration and environment minister Hussein Makhlouf decreed that only these wounded fighters and relatives of the dead were eligible to apply for permits to operate roadside kiosks, a ubiquitous type of small shop that sells cigarettes, SIM cards, candy, and newspapers in Syrian cities.[161] Privileges of this type are meaningful and tangible in a country where, as of 2016, six in ten citizens were estimated to live in extreme poverty.[162]

In sum, loyalist militia commanders have a strong incentive to ensure the formal legality of their groups and to win the favor of senior regime figures, since doing so allows themselves and their fighters to access the state's military, logistical, economic, and social support functions. Once again, the quest for legal status remains a key concern of hybrids, but in a context where the state has retained its practical and symbolic centrality, its ability to grant or withhold institutional legitimacy may serve as a constraint on their development.

Imperfect State Control

To date, there are no known instances of NDF units turning against the government as such, or adopting anti-Assad positions. There is, however, some evidence that the Syrian leadership has had to struggle to maintain discipline among local militias. Chiefly, this has been a problem of criminality, sectarian aggression, and local vendettas rather than military mutinies or political protest. Still, even these problems have been disruptive at times. In July 2013, for example, Alawite militants in the religiously mixed Talkalakh region reportedly killed seven members of a local reconciliation committee coming from a rebel-held Sunni Turkmen town nestled among Alawite and Shia villages. The dead included two retired SAA officers and a former village mayor, who had been trying to escort unarmed Sunni rebels wishing to surrender to the Talkalakh police station.[163]

Homs provides an example of how government plans were obstructed, or at least delayed, by hawkish NDF groups with vested interests in the war economy. After cornering opposition fighters in the Old City in 2012, the SAA and its militia allies in Homs put in place a siege that cut off access to food and medicine to starve out the insurgent enclave. Many of the checkpoints and positions surrounding the area were manned by Saqr al-Rustom's NDF fighters. Rustom's group appears to have profited from its control over whatever limited trade and traffic existed, and it grew so influential in Homs that its involvement became indispensable for any agreements between the government and the besieged rebels, according to a London School of Economics study based on interviews with local negotiators.[164]

In October 2013, a three-man team was delegated by the Homs rebels to seek a cease-fire on their behalf. The Syrian government received the group in Damascus, where it had a series of "encouraging" meetings with senior Syrian officials and with the Iranian embassy. Their government liaisons then informed the rebels that Assad had handed the issue to Bassam al-Hassan, who told the delegates to return to Homs and speak directly with Rustom. According to the rebel negotiators, Rustom proved more intransigent than his ostensible superiors. Although he accepted the idea of letting civilians leave the besieged area, he rejected the idea of a long-term ceasefire with the rebels, instead vowing to "crush them one by one." The talks ground to a halt.[165]

Nevertheless, the Homs rebels reached an agreement with the government a couple of months later, with the help of the United Nations. The agreement stipulated that the government allow both rebels and civilians to safely evacuate Homs to rebel-held regions further north, after which the Old City would return to government control. But when the deal began to be implemented, NDF members shelled a humanitarian corridor established by the United Nations and the Syrian Arab Red Crescent. The shelling was apparently an attempt to block the agreement's implementation. Assad ended up having to dispatch Maj. Gen. Mohammed Dib Zaitoun, the head of the General Intelligence Directorate, to impress on the NDF that the president wanted the deal to succeed.[166] As a postscript to the affair, NDF groups then briefly clashed with other loyalist fighters from the SSNP as both militias moved into the emptied Old City.[167] The conflict had an implicit sectarian dimension—in Homs, the NDF was virtually all-Alawite and the SSNP was in large part Christian—but more likely represented rivalries over loot and territory.

In spring and summer 2017, the Syrian president was again forced to send out Dib Zeitoun on a mission to rein in unruly militias—this time in Aleppo, where Sami Oubri's wing of the NDF was deeply embroiled in looting and organized crime. After retaking eastern Aleppo in December 2016, fighters from the NDF and other militias had continued to prey on local business, abuse civilians, and impose exorbitant "escort fees" on traffic and goods entering the city. Regime-connected businessmen repeatedly complained, and an influential member of parliament from Aleppo, Fares Shehabi, castigated the militiamen as "thieves, thugs, trash."[168] Dib Zeitoun was dispatched to Aleppo to oversee a clampdown, and the SAA's regional Security and Military Committee forced Oubri to hand over the NDF center to his former operations manager, Col. Emad Hassan.[169]

Tensions have also appeared within the NDF itself. In 2017, the new leader of the Homs center, Khaldoun Abu Ali, drifted into conflict with his predecessor, Rustom, who was then based at the NDF's General Secretariat. Details are scarce, but there appears to have been a power struggle: the General Secretariat reportedly had cut off salary payments to subcommanders loyal to Abu Ali, and Rustom stood accused of having ordered a failed attempt on Abu Ali's life. In a call-in interview with a Homs radio station, Abu Ali accused Rustom of thinking "he is the state in Homs," and erupted: "We didn't fight for a man like Saqr al-Rustom to come and lead a mafia with power and money and killing innocents."[170] It remains unclear how the affair ended.

Despite such examples of internal friction, the overall unity of the loyalist camp has remained impressively strong, and by 2019 the Syrian government's effort to maintain control over otherwise disparate militias appears to have been successful. Intra-loyalist rivalries certainly exist, but serious violent conflicts have been both brief and rare and typically appear to have been rooted in financial, personal, or clan rivalries. So far as it finds any expression at all in the public sphere (for example, online), intra-loyalist political criticism typically remains phrased in pro-regime terms—as an attack on corrupt figures cheating the system, rather than on the system itself.

Abu Ali's radio interview may illustrate the point. To publicly attack a powerful loyalist figure like Rustom was a flagrant breach of political etiquette in Assad-controlled Syria, where unsanctioned politics and open disagreements have been taboo since the Ba'ath Party seized power in 1963. But Abu Ali was careful to frame his criticism as an appeal to the state and the president. He framed Assad as a defender of lawful authority and institutional rule, in contrast to Rustom, whom he accused of illicit activities, abuse of power, and personal greed. Rhetorically, it resembled nothing so much as a provincial lord appealing to the king for redress against a transgressing rival.[171]

In sum, the NDF was, at its peak, a borderline hybrid actor, a fusion between a state-run project and nonstate elements that operated with private Syrian and foreign (Iranian) support. It still evinces some of the characteristics of a hybrid actor: it is a major security provider with some degree of financial autonomy from the government, and NDF leaders engage in the limited provision of services. Nonetheless, the NDF shows no sign of propagating a distinct ideology or of collective political ambition, and instances of NDF–state tension have been few and local in nature. Wary of the NDF's potential for divergence from state interests, the Syrian government has worked from the outset to counteract its evolution into a genuine, autonomous hybrid actor—first by channeling Iranian support and loyalist nonstate militancy into an SAA-linked framework, and subsequently by keeping the NDF structurally dependent on state services. Should the Syrian state weaken further, or if the Assad regime were to break apart at senior levels, the NDF's latent potential for autonomous evolution could swell quickly. As yet, no such conditions are on the horizon, but nevertheless it is a risk to which Syrian authorities seem well attuned.

Relationship with Patron (Iran)

Although Syrian officers and senior regime figures were instrumental in establishing the NDF and in leading its operations thereafter, the group would not have been created without support from Iran's IRGC. According to the U.S. government, by the end of 2012, shortly after the first elements of the NDF were formed, Iran was already providing "training, advice, and weapons and equipment" as well as "routine funding worth millions of dollars" to the emerging militia.[172] Some NDF recruits were even flown to Iran to attend specialized training programs, studying unconventional warfare at facilities that also appeared to be servicing Lebanon's Hezbollah.[173]

For a number of reasons, Assad's critics have tended to exaggerate Iranian influence in Syria, including in relation to the NDF. Exaggerating Iran's dominance in Syria has been a useful mobilizing tool for Syrian rebels, as it frames Assad as a puppet of foreign occupiers. It has also been a way to attract support from anti-Iranian and anti-Shia circles in the Sunni Gulf states, such as Saudi Arabia. Last but not least, the Iranian presence is a major driver of Israeli pressure on the regime and of U.S. involvement in Syria. Donald Trump's policy has been torn between two contradictory impulses: pulling U.S. troops out of Syria and remaining in Syria to pressure Iran.[174] Assad's government has, conversely, been keen to stress the NDF's Syrian character and downplay Iran's role.[175] At stake is the question of whether Iranian support for the NDF has also translated into Iranian proxy control. Given that both the Syrian security apparatus and the IRGC's external operations wing, the Quds Force, are notoriously secretive, it is unlikely that the exact backstory to the NDF's creation will ever be fully known. Some information has nevertheless filtered out, including in a posthumously published account by IRGC Brig. Gen. Hossein Hamedani.[176]

Until his death near Aleppo in October 2015, Hamedani was a key figure in the IRGC's Syrian operations. In interviews for a Persian-language book published after his death, excerpts of which are available in Arabic translation, Hamedani insists that Iran and Hezbollah were the primary drivers of the NDF project, against objections from suspicious, apathetic, and disorganized Syrian officials. In one passage, Hamedani describes traveling to Damascus alongside Quds Force leader Qasem Soleimani in January 2012. Once in Syria, the team continued to Homs and was introduced to Rustom and a local Shia cleric, "Sheikh Mohsen."[177] On the IRGC's urging, Rustom and the cleric recruited 2,000 Alawite and five hundred Shia fighters, who were armed and trained by the Iranians. The IRGC team then appears to have developed a more ambitious training program, but faced resistance from Syrian officials, who feared the consequences of a broad mobilization of the population, including Sunnis, and who were unwilling to let the Iranians work within the SAA. "We spoke to Mr. Bashar al-Assad," Hamedani is quoted as saying,

> and we agreed with him that we would first begin training the young men. If the army then saw a need for them, it could use them [in its own ranks] and they had to be fully prepared. The Syrian army was unable to conduct training because it was preoccupied with battles and was spread out across different regions. Therefore, we called on the youth to mobilize in the governorates of Damascus, Latakia, and Tartous, and a part of the Homs governorate that was under the control of the Syrian regime.[178]

However, according to Hamedani, the Syrian government continued to reject elements of the IRGC's plan. Frustrated at the lack of cooperation, the Iranians at one point asked to return home but were told to stay put by Iranian supreme leader Ali Khamenei. In a dramatic flourish, Hamedani reports that the full scope of his plan was approved by Assad only in March 2013, when, he says, the government was on its last legs:

> In March 2013, the terrorists were getting close to complete victory. They were receiving major support from Saudi Arabia, Qatar, the [United] Arab Emirates, and other Western states. The siege was being tightened to the point where it reached close to the Presidential Palace in Damascus, and they took over the areas around it. It was a very difficult night. We sent our family members to a safe location and Assad, who felt that the game was up, was thinking of escaping to another state.
>
> In the final proposal I made to Bashar al-Assad, I told him: "Now that we are close to seeing the Presidential Palace fall in opposition hands and everything is coming to an end, you must accept our proposal." He said: "What is that?" I said: "Open the weapon stockpiles to arm the

people, and they will repel those terrorists by themselves." He approved the proposal, and, thank God, on that night Syria was saved from certain defeat as the people expelled the takfiri terrorists from the surroundings of the Presidential Palace and went on to remove them from the cities. This force formed what is known as the National Defence Forces, which is today fighting Da'esh [the Islamic State] and the Nusra Front and the rest of them.[179]

Of course, Hamedani's account is impossible to take at face value. In several respects, it comes across as self-serving, for example by constantly stressing Iran's centrality and framing the IRGC, Khamenei, and Hezbollah as being wiser and more attuned to the reality in Syria than the Syrians themselves. Furthermore, there is certainly no evidence that the regime was days or weeks from collapsing in March 2013. That spring may well have been the lowest point of the regime's fortunes, and rebels were active in the capital's suburbs, but neither Damascus nor the Presidential Palace were, properly speaking, under siege. And although Hamedani's timeline roughly matches the known evolution of the NDF, it appears to place the launch of the project several months too late. It is clear that some NDF units had already formed in 2012, and the group was the subject of several media reports starting in January 2013.[180] However, the first instance of large-scale offensive action by NDF fighters seems to have happened during the April-May 2013 retaking of al-Qusayr, which also marked Hezbollah's officially recognized entry into the war. In terms of chronology, this development seems like a good fit with Hamedani's dramatized reference to Assad green-lighting some form of IRGC plan in March 2013.

Synthesizing Hamedani's narrative and other information, it is possible to form a reasonable (albeit speculative) hypothesis about the sequence of events. An IRGC team certainly could have arrived in Syria in January 2012, as Hamedani reported. It also is reasonable to assume that Hassan was assigned by Assad to facilitate the IRGC mission—even though Hassan does not appear to play any part in the Iranian narrative—given that he would later come to manage the Syrian end of the NDF project. Through Hassan, the IRGC effort would have been directed toward his nephew Rustom in Homs, which led to the training of an initial batch of fighters. The IRGC apparently wanted to keep building on this initial success, pitching a more ambitious plan for the widespread generation of militias and hands-on Iranian/Hezbollah involvement with the SAA's war effort. Per Hamedani's narrative, it met with resistance and foot-dragging from officials in Damascus. However, the IRGC and its Syrian partners nonetheless managed to stand up a proto-NDF branch in Homs in mid-2012 and later began to add new centers in Latakia, Damascus, and elsewhere. A partially built-out militia network seems to have been in place by early winter 2012. Final approval for additional elements of the Iranian plan, perhaps relating to full-blown Hezbollah intervention or other direct IRGC involvement, may (per Hamedani's narrative) have been held back until spring 2013, culminating in the Quseir operation. From that point on, through the beginning and middle of 2013, the NDF apparatus continued to expand across Syria.

Iran's Uncertain Continuing Role

In sum, Iran appears to have had a considerable role in the creation of the NDF. However, its subsequent influence over the organization is harder to pin down. In Lebanon and Iraq, the IRGC has been able to establish Shia Islamist groups that are ideologically and religiously linked to the Iranian leadership and its doctrine of the Rule of the Jurisprudent, but no such thing would have been possible with the NDF, whose recruits hailed from many different ethnic and religious groups but presumably were mostly Alawites invested in the Ba'athist order, few of whom would have had any interest in Islamist politics, Shia or otherwise. Further complicating matters for the IRGC—so far as it ever intended to turn the NDF into an Iranian proxy force—the Syrian government seems to have imposed tight control mechanisms on the NDF through leadership appointments and by keeping it structurally dependent on the SAA and the state.

As we have seen above, central elements of the project appear to have been steered by Hassan, a close collaborator of the president. The first batch of governorate-level NDF leaders seems to have been selected with a premium on trust and loyalty. Key posts were handed to relatives and friends of the Assad family and of Hassan, and SAA career officers appear to have filled many other positions. The default allegiance of such figures surely must have been to the Damascus government or to their patrons within the Syrian regime, and not to Iran. No less importantly, the NDF remained dependent on the SAA for logistical and other support, and ordinary NDF fighters continued to live with their families in areas ruled by the Syrian government, relying on the state for any number of mundane needs.

In other words, there is little to recommend the view that Iran "controls" the NDF in any meaningful sense, or that the IRGC leadership even had the ambition to do so. The primary objective of Iran's assistance to the Assad regime appears to have been to save it, not to cannibalize its remains—an objective that could have changed, however, had the state collapsed despite Tehran's best efforts. Even so, intense Iranian involvement with the NDF clearly created inroads for IRGC operatives, helping them gather sensitive information, build trust with key leaders, gain leverage over individual commanders or groups, and disseminate their messaging and ideology. The IRGC may also have drawn on NDF structures and cadres to support other Iranian-led projects in Syria. For example, a eulogy for former SAA Special Forces major Ahmed Maalla Maalla, published in the journal of the Syrian veterans' association, notes that he helped create the Tartous branch of the NDF, but goes on to explain that Maalla's "excellent reputation" led to him being called on to work directly with the "friendly forces"—a common euphemism for the IRGC and Hezbollah.[181] In fact, the NDF is far from the only group in Syria that Iran backs, and a separate network known as the Local Defense Forces (LDF, Quwat al-Difaa' al-Mahalli) seems to have an even closer relationship with the Iranians.[182] In seeming contrast to the NDF, for example, the LDF contains visibly Hezbollah-linked Shia factions, and there is at least some evidence of Shia proselytization in its ranks.[183]

IRGC leaders do appear to have pushed for the NDF's preservation and institutionalization in postwar Syria, presumably to retain access and influence. While Iran is normally careful not to visibly interfere in Syrian domestic affairs, Mohammed Ali Jafari, the IRGC commander at the time, reportedly spoke in favor of the permanent retention of the NDF in 2017, and said that Assad "knows the importance of the NDF and will surely make it legal in Syria"—in other words, a standing force—"in order to confront future threats."[184]

Iran's desire to maintain the NDF in postwar Syria is somewhat problematic for the Damascus leadership, as it struggles to recover from years of war. The United States, Israel, European nations, and the Arab states of the Gulf oppose Iran's presence in Syria. Some of these nations have also attempted to enlist Russia's services in rolling back Iranian influence in Syria, so far with little success.[185] To add a further layer of complexity, rising tensions in the Gulf and a tightening of U.S. sanctions on Iran may constrain Tehran's ability to support Assad's government in the future. Although Iran's connection to the NDF is hardly a central front in Tehran's conflict with Washington, it is nonetheless one piece of a larger puzzle that may influence the militia's future prospects in Syria.

In contrast to Lebanon's Hezbollah or groups within the Iraqi PMU, there is little evidence that the NDF meaningfully responds to Iranian directives over those of the Syrian government. It certainly is not a straightforward Iranian proxy. Instead, it represents a middle-way outcome between a state-run Syrian project and a hybrid actor as defined in this report. To fully attain hybrid actor status, the NDF would likely require sustained external support in a context of continued Syrian state disintegration, pulling its leaders deeper into governance and service provision. Absent such a situation, a more probable future is that the NDF will continue to be integrated into the SAA, perhaps with Russian support, while Iran shifts its attention toward smaller and more explicitly Tehran-aligned factions, which may be drawn from within the NDF, the LDF, or other militia constellations.

Amal of Lebanon

Lebanon's Amal movement debuted in 1975 as a precursor to Hezbollah, and for a time it thrived as a hybrid actor in parallel to Hezbollah. In the late 1980s, in fact, during the final stages of the Lebanese Civil War, Amal (with Syria's backing) fought a series of deadly battles against Hezbollah (with Iran's backing) in one of the more dramatic manifestations of war between hybrids with overt foreign backing. Yet by the 1990s, Amal had fully disbanded its militia, and staked its fate and that of its constituents on its role as a patronage-rich political party within the state. Amal and its constituency today depend on state riches to thrive. Amal's path has paralleled Hezbollah's; today, Amal often operates as Hezbollah's political partner. And though Amal's patronage and corruption pose yet another challenge to the viability of the Lebanese state, Amal still decisively supports Lebanon as a state. Amal does not directly promote the ambiguous state of fragmentation that best suits hybrids.

Although Hezbollah has become almost synonymous with Lebanese Shia politics in the international press, the militia-cum-political party is not the only representative of Shia political thought and action in Lebanon. The Amal party also continues to boast a large Shia constituency. Today, Hezbollah and Amal are almost always on the same side of politics in Lebanon; since 2005, they have run in joint electoral lists in local and national elections. Local news media outlets have dubbed them the "Shia duo."[186] But Amal is not a mere sidekick to Hezbollah. It is an actor in its own right, and in some sense continues to rival Hezbollah for the leadership of the Lebanese Shia community. What is distinct about Amal is that, unlike Hezbollah—and despite Amal's historical roots as a militia—it does not exhibit behavior or ambitions that would make it a hybrid actor. Rather, it has transformed into a political party that is fully invested in the Lebanese state. Though it depends heavily on patronage to maintain popularity with its constituency—and in doing so furnishes some services that a state traditionally provides—this is simply a hybrid-actor-like feature of the party. Amal does not directly provide security to its constituents, nor does it supplant or seek to replace the state.

History and Founding

In Lebanon's Shia community, Shia-dominated militias emerged before the establishment of Shia political parties—in contrast to the sequence of organization for other confessional groups, which were parties before they were militias.[187] At the outbreak of the Lebanese Civil War in 1975, the Shia community had long suffered from lack of political representation and power. During the early years of Shia mobilization of the 1980s, localized allegiances and a lack of solidarity among Lebanese Shia militias were commonplace. Amal originally was established as a Shia militia in July 1975—it predated Hezbollah, and its senior leaders, such as Husayn Musawi, were among the most notable Lebanese founders of Hezbollah. The party's name, which means "hope" in Arabic, is an acronym for Afwaj al-Muqawamah al-Lubnaniyah, or the Lebanese Resistance Detachment. Amal was the armed branch of popular Shia imam Musa al-Sadr's Harakat al-Mahroumin (Movement of the Deprived), which Sadr had established the previous year. Although the Movement was putatively nonsectarian, it had been founded by a prominent Shia cleric and launched at a rally in the Shia-dominated city of Baalbek, which left no doubt that the "Deprived" in its name referred to the Shia.[188]

Eventually, Amal subsumed the Movement as a military and political organization. Several events bolstered the new militia as the locus of Shia political expression in Lebanon. Among these events were the disappearance of Sadr in Libya in August 1978; the Israeli invasions of Lebanon in 1978 and in 1982; the 1979 Iranian revolution; and the growing disillusionment with the Palestine Liberation Organization (PLO), which many Shia viewed as having provoked Israeli attacks and invasions. Insecurity emerged as one of the biggest concerns of the Lebanese Shia community, and Amal attracted the Shia that had hitherto been drawn to nationalist and leftist parties. The organization garnered wide support, funds, and weapons, but its infrastructure remained relatively underdeveloped and its leadership structure weak.[189]

The leadership that replaced Sadr was nonclerical, and individual clerics had little to do with Amal's day-to-day operations.[190] Nabih Berri, who became the head of Amal after Sadr's disappearance in 1980 and has been the party's leader ever since (and the speaker of parliament since 1992), rejected the Islamic national model, and today still stresses the integrity of a multiconfessional Lebanese state.[191] In its 1983 convention, Amal reorganized its structure. It eliminated pro-Iranian elements that were critical of Berri's centrist policies, and deemphasized the military aspect of the organization to secure more economic gains and enhance the social standing of the Shia.[192] Amal sought to extend governmental authority and legitimate state governance and, in turn, extend its own authority through government bodies. Under Berri, Amal has worked with a spirit of pragmatism, attaining government positions, and distributing state patronage to its Shia constituency.

The Taif Agreement of 1989, which paved the way for the end of the civil war, required all militias to disarm, except for Hezbollah. Amal transformed entirely into a political organization, although one with a considerably muscular street presence. Amal has come to represent the more moderate, ostensibly leftist secular portion of Lebanese Shia politics. In its charter, Amal identifies as a nonsectarian, nationalist Lebanese movement that advocates secularism and supports the concept of Lebanese national sovereignty. Amal embraces Islam, but it is not an Islamist party, nor is it known for religious fanaticism. Instead, it professes the importance of Islam as a cornerstone of Arab civilization.[193] Whereas Hezbollah was established as a military organization opposing Israeli occupation, Amal, since its founding, has focused its efforts on pushing for institutional reform, and has supported the role of government in resource redistribution.

Its main success has been funneling state resources into the Shia community in the form of development funds, construction projects, education, and jobs. The movement has always sought to advance Shia interests, but within the framework of the Lebanese state. In distinction from Hezbollah, Amal is committed to Lebanon as a "distinct and definitive homeland," and has a thoroughly moderate religious character. [194] Amal has advocated a "general overhaul of the sectarian political system," whereas Hezbollah has held that no reform would solve this fundamentally oppressive structure of governance and that it must be uprooted.[195] Hezbollah and Amal have thus had opposing methodologies for change.

Amal does not appear to seek the same autonomy from the state that Hezbollah and other hybrid actors work to maintain. It does, however, enjoy several elements of hybridity. It indirectly provides protection and political cover for its constituencies, and provides social services from within and without state institutions. In doing so, Amal perpetuates the weakness of state policy and political structures. To retain these hybrid elements, Amal must maintain the confessional Lebanese state, despite the party's professed commitment to a nonsectarian order. Thus, Amal denounces confessionalism but still plays by the rules of confessional politics. However, unlike Hezbollah, Amal does not pledge allegiance to Ayatollah Ruholla Khomeini's Rule of the Jurist concept, which positions the Iranian supreme leader as the guide of Muslims everywhere. Instead, it explicitly limits its political program to the existing Lebanese nation and state structure, in its fragmented, penetrable form. It is unsurprising, then, that Amal's cooperation with Lebanon's political system has caused it to represent, in the words of security analyst Rodger Shanahan, "the very system it was set up to oppose."[196]

Relationship with Patron (Syria)

From its founding, Amal aligned itself with Syria, then led by Hafez al-Assad. In the early years of the Lebanese Civil War, Sadr gave his imprimatur to the Alawite sect (the sect to which Assad belonged) by acknowledging them as Muslims. This significantly boosted the prestige of the Alawites in the Muslim world, even though other clerics have denounced the sect's heterodox form of worship as being too distant from the teachings of Islam to be considered part of the religion, Shia or otherwise. Syria provided training for the Amal militia, as it did for other groups active in Lebanon, such as the PLO and Fatah. Even after the civil war ended in 1990, Berri maintained personal ties with Syrian figures such as Syrian vice president Abdul Halim Khaddam; chief of staff Hikmat al-Shihabi; and Maj. Gen. Ghazi Kanaan, head of Syrian military intelligence in Lebanon. Berri did Syria's bidding in Lebanon and, in return he reaped political benefits that allowed him to stay in parliament. For example, Syria pushed Hezbollah to form a joint electoral list with Amal when the latter's electoral victory was jeopardized in the 2000 parliamentary elections.[197]

After the end of the civil war, Amal, in coordination with Hezbollah, changed its focus from militia operations to alliance-making, constituent representation, and other activities common to political parties in parliamentary systems. In 2000, Bashar al-Assad became president of Syria, after his father's death. The new Syrian president grew closer to Nasrallah and weakened Berri's central role as Syria's connection. Still, Berri was careful to maintain a good rapport with Syria. Even after Syrian troops withdrew from Lebanon in April 2005, Berri continued to align with Hezbollah's pro-Syria Lebanon axis, and emphasized the importance of maintaining bilateral relations and diplomatic ties between the two governments.

Yet even though Berri maintained a close alliance with Syria, Amal was not a Syrian proxy, as more recent events have shown. Tensions have risen between Berri and the Syrian government since the outbreak in 2011 of the Syrian crisis.[198] Despite Hezbollah's military involvement in the Syrian war alongside the Syrian regime, Amal has followed Lebanon's "dissociation" policy. The policy, approved by the Lebanese cabinet in 2017, calls on "the Lebanese government, with all its components" to dissociate itself from any "conflicts, struggles, or wars, as well as the internal affairs of Arab countries to safeguard

Lebanon's political and economic relations with its Arab brothers."[199] The break with Syria was far from total. Although the policy of dissociation might seem to be a passive condemnation of the Syrian regime's behavior, it has in fact allowed Amal to avoid commenting on the events in Syria, even when they affected Lebanon. In 2012, the Amal-affiliated minister of foreign affairs and emigrants, Adnan Mansour, refused to send a letter of complaint to the Syrian government over border violation by Syria.[200]

As part of its pragmatism, Amal has always acknowledged the centrality of the Lebanon–Syria nexus. In his 1987 book, *Amal and the Shi'a*, Augustus Richard Norton wrote that Berri had a talent for "intentional indecisiveness" and a "policy penchant for keeping all options open.[201] This assessment is even truer today. By 2016, Amal had revived its ties with the Syrian government. Amal-affiliated minister of agriculture Ghazi Zaiter has visited Damascus twice since 2017, and Berri condemned the decision to exclude Syria from the 2018 Arab Economic Summit in Lebanon.[202] "I will not accept any Arab meetings without Syria," Berri said at the time.[203]

Relationship with the State (Lebanon)

Amal is fully integrated into the Lebanese state. It conducts certain activities outside of state systems to cater to its constituents, but it does not do so in competition with the state, and the party does not exhibit ambitions to replace the state. This stands in stark contrast to Hezbollah. Hezbollah participates in Lebanese state structures and politics, but this is the lesser part of its activities, and it seems to do so mostly as a way to hedge its bets and maximize its influence, and not because it is seeking to submit to the state, at least in the near term. Hezbollah has its own military, training grounds, and securitized zones in Lebanon, and intervenes in conflicts outside the country.

Hezbollah's power also gives it more muscle and control over the Shia street. Ever since Amal's relationship with Bashar al-Assad soured, some analysts have claimed that Amal depends on Hezbollah's electoral support for its survival. To some degree, Hezbollah's brawn also limits Amal's ambitions; the fact that observers often view the latter as a sidekick to the former says more about the power imbalance that has emerged than it does about Amal's ambitions and self-perception.[204] Hezbollah likewise needs Amal. As part of the "Shia duo," Amal acts as the domestic moderator to Hezbollah's transgressive actions. Amal helps represent Hezbollah's interests in the Lebanese government, and provides a more moderate option for a concerned Shia public.

Amal has maintained a relatively good standing for its constituency by manning ministerial posts, coopting state institutions and local agencies, and setting up its own nongovernmental social service network. Today, supporters of Amal are more interested in the party's patronage networks than in its ideological position. Whereas Hezbollah set up a social service network that is entirely parallel to the state's services, Amal uses a more diversified strategy. Amal saw state institutions and government positions as central to Shia social revival. Moreover, Amal supporters have huddled around the personality of Berri. Berri has been the leader of Amal since 1980, and Lebanon's speaker of parliament for almost three decades now—no small feat in an environment replete with bickering elites and political stalemate. Today, Berri is seen as the most important arbiter among Lebanon's sectarian political elite, and the only Shia politician that can calm public concern abroad over Hezbollah's actions.

Amal relies on a corrupt, sectarian, and regionalized political system that allows it to retain its hybrid elements. In this, it differs little from many other Lebanese political parties. It also shares these traits with Hezbollah: both control different municipalities and so oversee different development projects by international nongovernmental and governmental organizations that are compelled to channel their funds through local government institutions. Also, Berri has emphasized his version of Lebanese nationalism by appointing more Shia to key governmental positions and offices, and by using government budgets to reallocate funds for the development of the South and Bekaa regions.

Apart from state-related means for service delivery, Amal has set up a modest parallel social service network, mainly run by Berri's wife, Randa. In 1984, Randa established the Lebanese Welfare Association for the Handicapped (LWAH), a self-described nongovernmental organization.[205] As part of its activities, LWAH runs a sophisticated health care facility in the south of Lebanon called the Nabih Berri Rehabilitation Compound.[206] Berri's son Bassel Berri has recently become the chancellor of Phoenicia University, a newly registered private university that is widely viewed in Lebanon as being influenced by Amal.[207]

In contrast to true hybrid actors, Amal does not have an armed wing. Amal can provide social security for its constituency through nepotism, patronage, and clientelist networks, or neighborhood security through its strongmen. However, what Amal lacks in military power, it makes up for in street power. If necessary, Amal can deliver chaos, instability, and insecurity. In 2018, when one politician called Berri "a thug" in a video recording, Amal supporters took to the streets, burning tires and blocking roads. Amal did not face any official punishments or other repercussions from Lebanese security agencies for the disturbances.[208]

Amal provides a case study of an entity that has moved from being a nonstate actor with hybrid characteristics, as it was during the civil war, to being a political party that works almost entirely within the state's systems. Amal's patronage networks, provision of social services, and relations with a foreign government exceed most traditional notions of the role of political parties. But in the context of Lebanon, with its weak central government and profusion of powerful political parties—many of which have roots as militias—Amal's expansive behavior is not particularly unusual. The party has an enduring alliance with Hezbollah—a hybrid actor par excellence—and the vast majority of its constituents have the same sectarian identity as Hezbollah's. Still, these facts alone do not make Amal a hybrid actor, any more than other powerful political parties in Lebanon.

The Kurdish Parties of Iraq

The dominant Iraqi Kurdish parties operate a duopoly in Iraqi Kurdistan, a region that has possessed considerable autonomy from the central Iraqi government since the United States extended military protection to the area and its leaders in 1991. The Kurdistan Regional Government (KRG), established in 1992, constitutes a near-state or unrecognized state. Since 2003, it has engaged in a push-pull relationship with Baghdad as the KRG and the Iraqi national government struggle over legal authority and budgets. The dominant parties in the region, the Kurdistan Democratic Party (KDP) and the Patriotic Union of Kurdistan (PUK), operate as a type of hybrid actor in the context of an unrecognized state. They are similar political parties that have armed wings but also engage in economic and political affairs. They aspire to become state actors and have built state structures; at the same time, they benefit from the gray area between state and nonstate. For instance, the KDP and PUK largely have resisted integrating their armed forces into the KRG—their own government structures—revealing the difficulties in achieving a monopoly over violence in the region.

However, unlike the main hybrid actors in this report, the KDP and PUK are different insofar as they have formed their own de facto government, one that is relatively independent from the Iraqi government and enjoys enhanced constitutional rights under the post-2003 (asymmetrical) federalist structure of the Iraqi state. The KRG has many of the trappings of statehood. It has its own parliament and cabinet (resembling a state), governs a relatively defined territory and population, and has the ability to engage in foreign affairs. The KRG benefits from support and close relations with a surprising array of foreign governments, including the United States, Israel, Turkey, and Iran. It enjoys de facto authority over its territories, and at times extends its territory, such as when it conquered Kirkuk in August 2014 and managed to hold the city until October 2017. However, it is not a formally recognized state.

As such, the KDP and the PUK are hybrid actors in the context of their own unrecognized state as well as in the context of the Iraqi state. The KDP and the PUK refuse to submit completely to the KRG or the central government in Baghdad, keeping one foot outside the structures and maintaining informal economic and military structures. Some of these armed forces—known as peshmerga, which literally means "those who face death"—have integrated into formal KRG structures as part of the Regional Guard Brigades (RGBs) under the KRG's Ministry of Peshmerga or the KRG Ministry of Interior's military police, the Zeravani. Most of the peshmerga, however, remain part of either the KDP or the PUK. This resembles other hybrid actors such as the PMU, which often speak of integration but prefer to keep their power apart from state institutions that they do not trust. Notwithstanding these divisions in loyalty, it nevertheless is common today to refer collectively to the armed forces of Iraqi Kurdistan as a single "peshmerga."

Iraqi Kurdistan captured the attention of many politicians and citizens in Western capitals during the fight against the Islamic State. In the summer of 2014, as the Islamic State conquered much of northwestern Iraq, the KRG, under the leadership of the KDP and the PUK, looked to Washington and other Western capitals for help. The disaster presented an opportunity to put Kurdistan on the map and develop its fledgling state structure—two things that KDP and PUK leaders were eager to do. Their strategy involved stressing the fighting capability of their peshmerga forces. Even as the Iraqi military collapsed in battles against the Islamic State in 2014, Kurdish leaders argued that the eight peshmerga brigades remained intact and continued to prove crucial in the battle against the Salafi-jihadist group.[209]

This section focuses specifically on the KDP and the PUK with regard to the KRG. The two parties do not trust each other. That is one reason that neither fully submits to the KRG, even though both deeply participate in it. Submitting to the KRG would mean potentially submitting to the other side. In the 1990s, the PUK and KDP fought a civil war; in the aftermath, the security apparatus of Iraqi Kurdistan became more centralized under the KDP, and the PUK peshmerga was weakened. Nonetheless, during this period, the KDP and PUK peshmergas continued to control separate areas of Iraqi Kurdistan. The KDP is strongest in the governorates of Erbil, Duhok, and parts of Nineveh, whereas the PUK is strongest in the governorates of Sulaymaniyah, Kirkuk, and parts of Diyala. Despite multiple efforts to unify them, the two have remained fractioned.

Security

Both the KDP and the PUK provide security to their respective areas, bolstering their claim to speak on behalf of the residents. They rely on their independent armed forces. In 1946, Mullah Mustafa Barzani took control of the peshmerga when he became minister of defense and commander of the Kurdish Army in the short-lived Mahabad Republic, a Kurdish state carved out of Iran. Barzani's peshmerga was a cross-Kurdish tribal paramilitary organization. The peshmerga split in 1975, and the two resulting factions became the fighting forces of the two major Kurdish parties.[210] Each party also has its own intelligence service, the Parastin (KDP) and the Zanyari (PUK). These intelligence services are sophisticated and supported by international intelligence agencies, with which they worked closely during the fight against the Islamic State, for example.

For much of the second half of the twentieth century, the two parties effectively maintained security and de facto authority in Iraqi Kurdistan. Prior to the 1990s, however, these efforts were mostly covert, because international actors did not want to recognize the Kurdish authorities. In 1991, the United States, France, and the United Kingdom changed policies and pushed for the United Nations to establish a safe haven that would become Iraqi Kurdistan, formalizing the KDP and the PUK's authority

The KDP and PUK armed forces are equipped with heavy weapons, including artillery, tanks, personnel carriers, and antitank weapons. The peshmerga does not have its own air support and relies on rudimentary equipment. Following the U.S.-led invasion of Iraq in 2003, the peshmerga maintained their status of independence from the Iraqi government. Article 121 (5) of the Iraqi constitution states: "The regional government shall be responsible for all the administrative requirements of the region, particularly the establishment and organization of the internal security forces for the region such as police, security forces, and guards of the region."

The provision of security through the control of an armed group has proved essential for political power and maintaining constituencies and patronage networks in Iraqi Kurdistan. When the Change Movement (Gorran) emerged as a split from the PUK and formed as an opposition party in 2009, its leadership faced difficulties operating in politics, partly because it did not have a peshmerga force and could not provide security. Despite the split, the PUK sustained its popular legitimacy partly because it could still claim to enjoy coercive control. To further its claims to representation, KRG leadership wished to showcase its ability to provide stability and security in the precarious neighborhood.

Service Provision

Through the use of both the KRG and their own political party offices, the KDP and the PUK have institutionalized their service provision. On the formal KRG side, ministries such as agriculture and water resources, electricity, education, health, and planning provide for citizens and as such build constituencies.[211] KRG public spending is more than 50 percent of its budget.[212] Most of this spending pays the salaries of citizens, leading some to argue that the KRG is a bloated bureaucracy using salary payments to maintain legitimacy.

Over the years, the KDP and the PUK have worked to ensure economic self-sufficiency. The KRG's revenue streams are based primarily on oil sales ($7.9 billion in 2018) and payments from the government of Iraq ($2.4 billion in 2018).[213] To gain more economic independence, the KRG developed a pipeline from oil fields around Kirkuk that runs only through KRG territory toward Turkey.[214] This move ensured that the KRG could, to some extent, generate revenue without having to rely solely on payments from Baghdad. The KDP and PUK peshmerga also collects revenue from a variety of sources, including taxation at checkpoints and many businesses inside and outside Iraqi Kurdistan.[215]

Like other hybrid actors, the KDP and the PUK rely on ideology to cement power. In this case, the use of Kurdish nationalism allows the groups to maintain a following, positioning themselves as the leaders of the Kurdish cause and against Baghdad. When their legitimacy is under threat and their constituents grow restless, the groups fall back on nationalism to shore up their appeal. For instance, following the fight against the Islamic State, the KDP leadership pushed for an independence referendum. Although the referendum was nonbinding and it was already clear from a similar referendum in 2005 that the Kurds wanted independence, the leadership used the vote to regain a sense of nationalism. As a result, its constituents were reminded of the KDP's role in the historic fight for Kurdish rights. The referendum helped successfully head off a popular challenge from Gorran that would have upended the long-standing political balance in Iraqi Kurdistan. PUK and KDP constituents rallied around the flag to reassert their support for the KRG and its parties.[216]

Foreign Affairs

The KDP and the PUK also engage in foreign affairs, both via the KRG as well as political parties in their own right. In 2014, as the Iraqi armed forces collapsed and retreated in the face of the Islamic State onslaught, the KDP and PUK leadership sought to develop the peshmerga as the West's main ally in the fight against the self-styled caliphate. Iraqi Kurdistan's chief of staff, Fuad Hussein, cited the weakness of the Iraqi armed forces when speaking to American officials less than a month after the Islamic State had captured Mosul: "80 percent of the Iraq army has collapsed," he said.[217] His point, it seemed, was that the West should support the Kurdish groups as the more trustworthy and effective ally.

Many Western leaders turned to the Kurdish peshmerga as an official state ally. Even Germany went against its traditional reluctance to participate militarily in international conflict and provided the peshmerga with the MILAN antitank rocket. During a press conference in Erbil with German defense minister Ursula von der Leyen, KRG president Masoud Barzani (2005–17) claimed that German support was integral for the peshmerga in its fight against the Islamic State.[218] Various foreign capitals now engaged openly with the KRG and provided the Kurdish groups with training and weapons. Not only did the West rely on the peshmerga to fight the Islamic State in Iraq, but Western governments also helped send KDP peshmerga to fight in Syria, as part of the battle for Kobani in September 2016.

In sum, the KDP and the PUK are noteworthy case studies because they resemble hybrid actors: they are political parties that operate inside and outside state institutions to engage in political, security, economic, and social affairs. Although both parties have worked to develop the trappings of statehood, the KRG is not a state. The Iraqi constitution grants the federal government exclusive authority over "formulating and executing national security policy, including establishing and managing armed forces to secure the protection and guarantee the security of Iraq's borders and to defend Iraq."[219] However, the KDP and the PUK have weakened the KRG's statehood by their refusal to submit their capabilities, power, and legitimacy to the KRG, instead keeping most to themselves. As such, they compete and cooperate with the state (in this case, the de facto state), matching this report's definition of the hybrid actor but in the context of an unrecognized state. In this sense, they are hybrid actors with regard to both the KRG and the government of Iraq.

The Iraqi Awakening

The Iraqi Awakening (in Arabic, the Sahwa) refers to a multiyear, broad-based realignment of Sunni tribal groups and former insurgents that saw former opponents of the United States turn against the

Islamic State in Iraq (ISI)—the successor to al-Qaeda in Iraq (AQI), which officially dissolved in October 2006. The manner in which that process evolved varied and depended on the time, place, and manner in which those shifts took place. As they took sides against ISI, these groups began fighting alongside and receiving support from the U.S. military. At its peak in 2008, the Awakening movement is estimated to have included nearly 100,000 fighters. With considerable credibility as a result of their military achievements, significant resources based on their partnership with the U.S. military, a constituency eager for effective representation, and a political vacuum stemming from the violence and chaos of the war, the Awakening and its key figures seemed well positioned to transform those assets into durable hybrid power. However, as this case study shows, the movement ultimately fell short of achieving hybrid actor status.

The Organic Emergence of a Movement

The initial realignment emerged organically, and began before the 2007 U.S. troop surge ordered by the George W. Bush administration, when Sunni tribes in Ramadi started actively organizing and fighting against AQI. Though the Awakening first emerged in Ramadi, its immediate successes encouraged both the U.S. military on the ground and Sunni tribal and insurgent leaders to replicate the model elsewhere in Anbar governorate. The bottom-up nature of the U.S. military effort was heavily influenced by the dire security situation in the governorate, which the U.S. Marine Corps' intelligence chief had described in 2006 as having been "lost" by the United States.[220] In an introduction to the official U.S. Marine Corps anthology of U.S. and Iraqi perspectives on the Anbar Awakening, the authors described it as an "indigenous movement to partner with U.S. forces to rid the region of al-Qaeda in Iraq [that] grew over time from multiple sources, coalesced in mid-2006, and blossomed in 2007."[221]

As a result of the movement's success, the United States sought to extend the Awakening model to Baghdad and other areas of the country with more diverse populations than Anbar, with its overwhelmingly Sunni Arab population. As the United States recruited new fighters elsewhere in the country, often engaging directly with former insurgents, it formalized these contacts and began referring to these groups as the Sons of Iraq. Owing to the imprecision with which the terms were used, even by U.S. military leaders, there is some confusion as to the relationship between the Awakening and the Sons of Iraq. In general, it is fair to say, as Najim Abed Al-Jabouri and Sterling Jensen have written, that "the Anbar Awakening and the Sons of Iraq program were two different initiatives, the former an Iraqi initiative and the latter an American one."[222] As of October 2008, there were 94,000 fighters in the Sons of Iraq program.[223] Among Iraqis, however, such distinctions were ignored, and the groups were referred to as Awakening groups regardless of geographic location.

The United States led the process to replicate the Awakening; it did not arise from agreements between the U.S. and Iraqi governments. As such, the Awakening groups operated outside central government authority, and as the movement expanded in mixed areas of Iraq, the Shia-led political order in Baghdad viewed it with skepticism. With an eye toward future withdrawal, the United States was keen to reach agreement with Iraq on future support for such groups more broadly, seeing them as a key to sustaining security gains. The United States eventually reached agreement for Iraq to integrate 20 percent of the fighters into its official military, with the remaining fighters vetted for other civil service positions or provided training to allow for transition into other employment.[224] In October 2008, as part of the broader transition toward full Iraqi assumption of security control and U.S. withdrawal, Iraq began incrementally assuming responsibility for the Awakening fighters.

Following the military success of the Awakening, the armed actors who directed the turn against ISI sought to parlay their military achievements into informal and formal political power. As the Iraqi civil war receded, the Awakening and its leadership seemed well positioned to fill the political vacuums that had emerged in

Sunni-majority areas of the country and to act as a political coun-terweight in other, mixed areas of the country. However, despite the myriad failures of the Iraqi state, the Awakening failed in its attempts to influence political life and institutionalize political power among Iraq's fragmented Sunni community. Further, its inability to continue to project military power ensured that the coalition of groups would not be able to function as a sustainable and effective hybrid actor, despite the temporary backing and assistance it received from the United States.

The Awakening was composed of widespread and separate groups of local actors with no broader organizational structures and no formal connectivity binding them together. Initially, their unify-ing motivation was a reaction against the advance of AQI. As one-dimensional as this purpose was, it marked a momentous shift in the dynamics of the war. Later, the broader fight against the Islamic State represented a struggle that most Iraqis and their leaders finally could agree on, across lines of sect. As a result, the rise of the Awakening helped to reduce violence in the country—violence that stemmed from both the civil war and the anti-U.S. insurgency—and seemed to portend an important political opening for Iraqis. That political opening, however short-lived, allowed for the hesitant exploration of cross-sectarian politics and the possibility of loosening the country's rigid ethnosectarian political framework.

This major shift in the trajectory of violence and the changing political climate that emerged with the Awakening also set in motion a prolonged discussion and debate within the U.S. military and among U.S. national security experts as to the causes of the reduction in vio-lence. The American views that emerged from these discussions were often simplistic and blinkered, focusing on troop increases, changing tactics, and steadfastness. These shallow analyses played a large part in distorting U.S. military thinking and planning.[225] The relative suc-cess of the Awakening convinced some U.S. military planners that they had unlocked a more appropriate method for engaging nonstate actors not only in Iraq but also in other conflict settings. Soon after, as U.S. attention was shifting to the war in Afghanistan, similar arguments were deployed in support of launching Afghan tribal militias as a supplement to U.S. and Afghan conventional forces.

Unexpected New Alliances

The Awakening's initial cooperation with U.S. forces came as a surprise to American and Iraqi officials alike. In the aftermath of the 2003 invasion, Anbar had gained a reputation as a hotbed of resistance to the U.S. occupation. But the various conflicts that had ravaged Anbar governorate since the invasion soon changed many local leaders' calculus about relations with the foreign army. First, within Anbar, AQI was threatening tribal leaders' power. "It had begun to push them aside," writes military analyst Carter Malkasian, "edging in on their territory and cutting into their smuggling business."[226] The nonaligned Sunni tribes also became direct targets of AQI, as the latter sought to establish its supremacy within the Sunni-majority areas of the country. More broadly, the sectarian civil war, as opposed to the anti-U.S. insurgency, had become the most immediate threat to the country's minority Sunni community, particularly in mixed areas. Moreover, Iraq's Sunnis had effectively lost that war and suffered unsustainable casualties in the process.[227] This stark reality shifted the calculation for many Sunni fighters who had been involved in both the insurgency against the United States and the sectarian civil war.

The political challenges for Iraq's Sunnis in the post-2003 political order were complicated by their previous role under Saddam Hussein's Ba'athist regime and their lack of political organization following Saddam's fall. Beyond their collective reservations and skepticism toward the country's emerging post-Ba'ath politics, Iraq's Sunnis were not prepared to contest political power, particularly as a distinct minority. Their lack of preparation stood in distinction to Iraq's Shia and Kurds, who had organized in exile over many years.[228] The de-Ba'athification process, which disproportionately affected Iraqi Sunnis, compounded the predicament. The question of Sunni political participation and representation became a major feature of the early years of the post-Saddam order. Even though every post-Ba'ath government included Sunni representation, broad swaths of the Sunni community nonetheless felt that they had been excluded from the new Iraqi political order. Neither did that representation provide effective political leadership on the particular issues that affected Iraq's Sunnis and animated their grievances with the new political dispensation.[229] In the words of Iraqi constitutional lawyer Zaid al-Ali, the exercise of "merely ensuring that there are ministers from each of Iraq's main communities—Shiites, Sunnis, Kurds and minorities like the Chaldeans and Turkmen[s]—will not ensure that they will represent those communities' interests, let alone the national interest."[230]

The expansion of the Awakening and the heightened U.S. political pressure for formal integration of the Awakening into the security organs of the Iraqi state and for a broader national reconciliation process seemed to augur a new opportunity for Iraqi Sunnis—a respite from the serial catastrophes of the post-Saddam era. With their newfound clout derived from their tactical achievements against ISI, informal forms of authority, and patronage sources, the Awakening appeared ready to grasp that opportunity. In the 2009 provincial elections, political parties and candidates linked to the Awakening performed well and were able to capture a significant share of representation in Anbar.[231] Writing in 2009, military and security analyst Michael Knights described an armed group coalescing around an identity of hybridity with both informal and formal means of advancing their political interests:

> The last twelve months have witnessed the Awakening movements being absorbed into a range of official political and security institutions of the Iraqi state. Sahwa leaders have been incorporated into a strengthening web of local government institutions such as District Development Forums and Neighborhood Advisory Councils. Many Sahwa leaders participated in provincial elections in

January 2009; the most successful Sahwa candidates were in Anbar, where Sheikh Abd al-Jabbar al-Rishawi (known as Jabbar Abu Risha) led the Iraq Awakening Council to a leading position on the provincial council.[232]

A Fleeting Political Opportunity

For the Awakening groups, however, this political opening was short-lived, undermined by Iraqi political and geographical realities and the finite nature of outside assistance and support from the United States. Initially, the Iraqi central government had a mostly positive perspective on the Anbar Awakening, owing to Anbar's unique status as Iraq's only Sunni-majority governorate and the obvious security gains achieved by the effort. The government did not reject the prospect of integrating the Anbar members of the Awakening into the Iraqi security forces: it was thought that Awakening groups' local focus did not represent a political threat to Baghdad.[233] But when the Awakening expanded beyond Anbar, the central government and Iraq's key political players took a sharply different view of the movement.

When Baghdad began to take steps to curtail the influence of Awakening groups in mixed areas of the country, it constantly emphasized the ways in which Anbar was different. In 2009, following a series of high-profile arrests of Awakening figures, Ministry of Defence spokesman Maj. Gen. Mohammed al-Askari lauded the Awakening in Anbar. He argued that it was a reaction to the rise of the Islamic State, and emphasized that its efforts represented a basis for political reconciliation. But he also went on to describe branches in other governorates as "harboring an ulterior motive—the desire to take advantage of incorporation into the security apparatus in order to assist those still intent upon carrying out guerrilla operations."[234] Similarly, Vice President Adel Abdul Mahdi (who would later become prime minister) described Awakening groups with suspicion. "Certain groups took up the Sahwa banner, in Baghdad and elsewhere, even some terrorist groups," he said. "Sometimes we can't distinguish between the two—the original Sahwa and the falsely

created Sahwa. The pretend Sahwa [is] these groups who are wait-
ing for the right moment to strike."[235] Brig. Gen. Nasir al-Hiti, commander of the Muthanna Brigade in Abu Ghraib, described members
of the Awakening as "like cancer" that the Iraqi government had
to remove. As late as 2010, and despite his government's hesitant
approach to the Awakening, then prime minister Nouri al-Maliki
distinguished among the groups. "We all know that this blessed phenomenon started in Anbar," he said. "Whenever the patriotic forces
and the tribes combine forces in the name of national security, victory comes."[236]

The government's stark hostility to Awakening groups that
emerged beyond Anbar ensured that they would not be provided
with an alternative source of patronage once U.S. support reached
an endpoint. Although the security gains proved beneficial at both
a local and national level, the Iraqi state did not understand its relationship with these groups as one of dependence. Baghdad was not
only unwilling to provide such support, but also opposed the groups'
existence and launched various crackdowns meant to quash them.

Diminishing U.S. Support Heralds Demise

The finite nature of U.S. support was perhaps the critical factor in the
eventual failures of the Awakening to sustain its military power and
extend its political influence. In addition to providing military support and assistance, U.S. forces also sought to enhance their clients'
economic self-sufficiency by awarding different types of contracts to
their new security partners. Through military mechanisms such as
the Commander's Emergency Response Program, the Department of
Defense streamlined this process and created the basis for patronage
networks that enhanced the reputation and clout of U.S. clients.

Following its withdrawal from Iraq in 2010, the United States
had no feasible means of continuing to provide military support to
its armed nonstate Sunni allies without the explicit permission of the
Iraqi government—which had no interest in allowing such arrangements to continue. "When we had a large military presence there

used to be a U.S. colonel with every Sunni tribe, but we couldn't sustain that kind of contact from the embassy in Baghdad," said former U.S. ambassador to Iraq James Jeffrey in 2014, describing this inevitable change. "It's also very tricky for the embassy, because we are diplomats and guests in Iraq by the permission of the government, and they didn't think we were there to run around with the Sunni tribes."[237]

On a political level, the demographic distribution of Iraq's Sunnis also hindered their ability to politically organize in an effective way. Other than in the overwhelmingly Sunni Anbar governorate, Iraqi Sunnis are, in the words of the International Crisis Group, "a heterogeneous, plural community, spread over provinces" and "encompass several confessional and ethnic groups."[238] It did not help that Awakening groups lacked an ideological orientation beyond the localized instrumentalization of tribal and sectarian identity. The Awakening also did not have any strong ideological overlap with either its patron or the government of its own country. It shared with Washington an antipathy to ISI, but little else, and faced deep-seated mutual mistrust and a fundamental divergence in political aims with Baghdad. Without a coherent political structure, enduring foreign or domestic backing, and the means to provide patronage, these local actors were unable to sustain their immediate hold on power or expand their profile.

Though the Awakening's failures were most acute outside of Anbar, they also were evident in the governorate from which the movement arose—a territory that had seemed to possess some of the components necessary to allow the Awakening to emerge as a credible, sustainable hybrid actor. The United States had been concerned about the eventual fate of the Awakening, specifically in how the Shia-led central government might treat it following a U.S. drawdown. Those concerns mounted with the slow pace of integration and the erratic and incomplete nature of payments for Awakening members. To remain relevant to Baghdad following the U.S. withdrawal, Awakening groups would have needed a grounding in local influence and power. But Awakening figures, crippled by fragmentation and a lack of formal political organization, fared poorly in the 2010 parliamentary elections. Deprived of external backing and receiving only limited support from the central government, even the groups in Anbar receded in terms of presence and relevance.

Two additional factors helped fatally weaken the Awakening in Anbar. First, Maliki's increasingly sectarian and centralizing impulses produced a backlash among Iraq's Sunnis that generated protests throughout Anbar. The rise of the protest movement created a dilemma for Anbar's tribal leaders, as Malkasian writes:

> Most of Anbar's tribal leaders backed the protests, yet in doing so they weakened their own control. They depended on the government for money, salaries, and privileges, but the protests forced them to choose between abandoning these perks or being discredited in the eyes of their tribesmen. And by accepting the legitimacy of mass political activity, the tribal leaders implicitly undermined their own authority. This enabled AQI supporters who had formerly been under the tribal thumb to come out, rally the people, and implicitly challenge the leaders who were now bereft of government support.[239]

As the insurgency regenerated and gathered force, the Awakening and its tribal leadership also became a prime target for what came to be known as the Islamic State, which undertook a coordinated and targeted assassination campaign against key Awakening figures.[240]

The cumulative effect of these various challenges and setbacks was the eventual demise of the Awakening as a political and military force. "We cannot fight them now," lamented an Anbari tribal leader in 2013, speaking in 2013, as the Islamic State gained military momentum. "They will kill us and get revenge because we fought them with American support. Today this government is not able to protect or support us."[241] By the time of the Islamic State's breakout military offensive in Anbar in 2014, tribal forces were no longer a

credible fighting force that could stem the momentum of the revital-
ized group. Despite belated attempts by Baghdad to revitalize tribal
forces after the fall of key urban areas in the governorate, the efforts
produced little: the Awakening was "dead."[242]

Although the Awakening briefly appeared on a trajectory to survive as a powerful, U.S.-backed Sunni hybrid actor in a Shia-centric
Iraq, its quick demise illustrates the fluid nature of armed groups in
fragile conflict zones. In particular, the Awakening experiment was
hampered by the evaporation of foreign support from the United
States, and by frontal pressure from the Iraqi state.

The Islamic State

The Sunni jihadist organization known as the Islamic State (also
known by the deliberately derogatory Arabic acronym, Da'esh) is difficult to fit into existing theoretical models. It has operated neither as
a normal nonstate actor nor as a proxy of another government. But it
is not a normal state entity, nor, properly speaking, is it a hybrid actor
of the type investigated in this report. The Islamic State has combined
typical nonstate actor practices with ideas explicitly antithetical to the
state system. At the same time, however, the Islamic State has shown
fairly advanced state-like governance and a religiously inspired ideology that, with its strong, idiosyncratic notions of statehood and sovereignty, distinguishes it from al-Qaeda-style Salafi-jihadism. In the eyes
of Islamic State leaders themselves, their "caliphate" is in fact not only
a state, but the world's only legitimate state—it is all other governments that have rebelled against the divine order that the Islamic State
seeks to uphold and embody. The territorial rise and fall of the Islamic
State's caliphate helps clarify the hybrid concept by its difference: the
Islamic State stepped out of the hybrid category through its quest to
perform statehood exclusively on its own terms.

The group was originally created as the Islamic State of Iraq
(ISI) in 2006, by al-Qaeda's Iraqi franchise and several smaller Iraqi
Sunni insurgent groups.[243] After repeated setbacks and losses in the

2007–10 period, ISI began to recover and expand into Syria in 2011, initially under the cover of a front group, the Nusra Front. In 2013, a messy internal split saw ISI rebrand itself as the Islamic State in Iraq and the Levant (often known as ISIL or ISIS), which would operate openly in both countries. Dissident members in Syria retained the Nusra Front moniker and pledged allegiance directly to al-Qaeda's international leader, Ayman al-Zawahiri, instead of the Islamic State leader, Abu Bakr al-Baghdadi.[244] Over the following year, the Islamic State drifted into violent conflict with other Syrian rebels and jihadists, including its erstwhile allies in the Nusra Front and al-Qaeda.[245]

In mid-2014, the group, still calling itself ISIS, capped a series of military victories with a declaration that Baghdadi had been anointed caliph of the Islamic world. The group's name was shortened to the Islamic State, reflecting its new claim to unrestricted sovereignty over the world's Muslims, and apocalyptic and messianic themes began to surface in the group's propaganda.[246] (For ease of reading, this case study henceforth uses the name "Islamic State" for the group for the entirety of its history.) In Fallujah, Raqqa, Mosul, and other Syrian and Iraqi cities, the Islamic State established a durable, state-like monopoly of force through startling displays of brutality. As its international notoriety grew, the group won new adherents across the world, with independent Salafi-jihadist organizations and al-Qaeda dissidents pledging allegiance to Baghdadi as far off as in Afghanistan, Libya, and Nigeria.[247]

As it turned out, however, declaring war on the entire world had its drawbacks. Under fire from several intervening nations, including the United States, Iran, Turkey, and Russia, the group's fortunes have declined since 2015. Nearly all of the ostensible caliphate in Syria and Iraq had been lost by 2017, and U.S.-backed Kurdish forces crushed the last Islamic State enclave in Syria in early 2019. However, even as a fugitive hiding in areas controlled by others, Baghdadi continued to style himself caliph and the Islamic remained committed to the improbable vision of itself as a "state" ("dawlah") rather than a mere "group" ("jama'ah").[248]

Pretensions to Statehood

Being a state implies a claim on sovereign control, which leaves little room for groups working outside the Islamic State system. From its perspective, such groups are nonstate actors. In practice, however, the Islamic State view of other Sunni jihadists has varied over time, reflecting not only a shifting context but also the group's internal evolution.

The group's early "state" in Iraq appears to have handled like-minded organizations pragmatically if often brutally. Sunni Islamist factions were encouraged to join the state project, sometimes through threats and violence, and ruthlessly persecuted if they tried to actively oppose it. However, the early Islamic State in Iraq did not, in general, portray the separate existence of such groups as a punishable affront in and of itself, and it had no quibble with the idea of other groups operating beyond Iraq. Although this early incarnation of the group was no longer an official al-Qaeda branch—al-Qaeda's Iraqi cadre had officially dissolved into the newly declared state in 2006—it maintained a collaborative relationship with al-Qaeda's international leadership and appears to have recognized the latter's primacy outside Iraq.[249]

"The relationship of the Islamic State with the jihadist groups, and especially with our brethren in the Ansar al-Islam group [in Iraq], is a solid relationship," explained an Islamic State official in an article published in 2008, when the group was far weaker than at its apex six years later. "The bond is one of method ["manhaj"] and creed ["aqidah"], and we are all in the same trench. There is intelligence and military cooperation, and although we desire a unification of the ranks and encourage groups to pledge allegiance to the Islamic State, it isn't an obstacle to working with our beloved brothers, the truthful mujahideen, and we would not deny their virtues in this blessed jihad."[250] In practice, members of other Iraqi insurgent groups, like Ansar al-Islam or the Islamic Army, complained that the Islamic State in Iraq treated them arrogantly and brutally, including by arresting and assassinating their leaders, and they often repaid such offenses in kind. These skirmishes probably had as much to do with the cutthroat nature of Iraqi insurgent politics as with the Islamic State's particular ideological pretensions.[251]

In post-2011 Syria, too, Islamic State operatives at first worked pragmatically and covertly within a factionally diverse Sunni rebel and Islamist movement. The idea that the "state" operated on a higher level of legitimacy than its allies resurfaced in April 2013, when Baghdadi dropped the Nusra Front cover, changed his group's name to the Islamic State in Iraq and Syria, and revealed the group's presence in Syria. But even then, Baghdadi said the Islamic State would "extend our wide hands and open our arms and hearts to the factions doing jihad for the sake of Allah Almighty and the proud tribes," inviting them to join without threatening punishment if they did not.[252] In this spirit of collaboration, Islamic State fighters at first fought side by side not only with the rump Nusra Front splinter and other Syrian Salafis, such as Ahrar al-Sham, but even with U.S.-backed fighters operating under the Free Syrian Army banner.

However, as competition with al-Qaeda and other rebels intensified through 2013, the Islamic State in Iraq and Syria retreated deeper into its idea of privileged statehood. Rival groups now found that the Islamic State rejected the insurgency's normal mechanisms for conflict resolution, such as joint sharia tribunals and arbitration by independent religious scholars. The Islamic State argued that, as a state, only its own courts had jurisdiction over its internal affairs. To allow nonstate groups any say in the matter would be to "infringe on the right of the Muslim sovereign and his state."[253] This attitude prevented easy resolution of local conflicts and poisoned the overall mood. In January 2014, full-scale civil war erupted among the insurgents, and the Islamic State broke away irrevocably from the rest of the rebellion. The resulting polarization between figures that supported either the Islamic State or al-Qaeda and the Nusra Front accelerated the Islamic State's drift toward ever more maximalist ambitions and a fixation with its own nature as a state.

On June 29, 2014, the declaration of Baghdadi's caliphate ended any lingering ambiguity as the Islamic State took its claim to divinely inspired statehood to its logical end point:

> We clarify to the Muslims that with this declaration of [a caliphate], it is incumbent upon all Muslims to pledge allegiance to [Baghdadi] and support him (may Allah preserve him). The legality of all emirates, groups, states, and organizations, becomes null by the expansion of the [caliphate]'s authority and arrival of its troops to their areas. . . . As for you, O soldiers of the [rebel and jihadist] platoons and organizations, know that after this consolidation and the establishment of the [caliphate], the legality of your groups and organizations has become invalid.[254]

The declaration of a caliphate extinguished all possibilities of compromise or hedging. Rival groups now had to make a choice between submitting to Baghdadi or entering into conflict with his followers.

Many Syrian and Iraqi Sunni Islamists chose the former and joined the Islamic State, believing it to be the safer bet: Baghdadi's group had just conquered Raqqa and Mosul, was unprecedentedly powerful, and treated rivals with blood-curdling cruelty. Those who continued to reject the group responded angrily to Baghdadi's perceived usurpation of Islamic legitimacy. "The reality of this so-called state, or the so-called caliphate, is that it rules by power and oppression," warned the Syrian Muslim Brotherhood.[255] "The restoration of an Islamic caliphate is a prophecy of the Prophet Mohammed, peace be upon him, but we don't believe that it has any relationship with the [Islamic State] declaration," said Hassane Abboud, the head of Ahrar al-Sham.[256]

Internationally, most well-known jihadist scholars denounced the Islamic State caliphate as "premature, ill-prepared, illegitimate, and generally a bad idea at this time and in the hands of al-Baghdadi," according to the Dutch academic Joas Wagemakers.[257] However, for a younger and more action-oriented generation of jihadist radicals, raised on Internet lectures and YouTube combat videos, Baghdadi's decision to implement divine law here and now proved irresistible.[258] Thousands of new recruits began flooding in from the Arab world and Europe to join the Islamic State, tipping the global intrajihadist balance of power away from al-Qaeda for the first time since the September 11, 2001, attacks.

The Islamic State's Governance

The Islamic State matched its claim to statehood with a dedicated effort to govern captured areas in a state-like fashion. Between 2014 and 2017, and even later, the Islamic State "built a state of administrative efficiency that collected taxes and picked up the garbage," wrote journalist Rukmini Callimachi after a *New York Times* examination of thousands of Islamic State documents captured in Iraq.[259] Its authorities issued marriage certificates, regulated market prices, registered vehicles, banned trademark infringements, and organized school exams. They also ran the armed forces, the police, prisons, and courts, and performed other basic state functions.[260]

For as long as it lasted, and on its own extreme terms, the Islamic State's state-building project appeared remarkably successful. However, it was not all Baghdadi's doing, as the Islamic State relied heavily on inherited administrative tools. The Sunni rebel factions that preceded the Islamic State in Syria had shown little talent for governance, typically looting public institutions when entering an area and jostling with each other over spoils and power. In sharp contrast to their predecessors' anarchic and short-termist behavior, the Islamic State made a point of reviving captured state institutions and dragging employees back to work, while also putting its own ideological stamp on their activities.[261] In Mosul, the Iraqi government's Directorate of Agriculture was kept operational but rebranded as the caliph's Diwan of Agriculture and brought into conformity with the Islamic State version of sharia law—female employees were fired, men were told they could no longer shave their beards, and meteorological services were shut down since rain is "a gift from God." However, captured institutions also were increasingly directed to carry out money-making schemes to fill Islamic State coffers, such as sales of confiscated Christian and Yazidi homes and farmland.[262]

The quest for financing and resources was a constant concern, and the economy was the area where the Islamic State most resembled "hybrid" nonstate actors that operate inside or alongside a state.[263] To secure profits from Syrian oil and gas installations, Islamic State leaders made pragmatic under-the-table deals with middlemen connected to the Damascus government, rival Sunni rebel groups, and even Western companies.[264] Institutional funding and public sector salary payments from the Iraqi and Syrian governments provided additional income and helped sustain governance functions in territory under Islamic State control.[265] After the Iraqi government cut off salary payments to Islamic State–controlled regions in mid-2015, the group became more dependent on tax collection—an area in which it showed real talent. As Callimachi writes:

> Ledgers, receipt books and monthly budgets describe how the militants monetized every inch of territory they conquered, taxing every bushel of wheat, every liter of sheep's milk and every watermelon sold at markets they controlled. From agriculture alone, they reaped hundreds of millions of dollars. Contrary to popular perception, the group was self-financed, not dependent on external donors.
>
> More surprisingly, the documents provide further evidence that the tax revenue the Islamic State earned far outstripped income from oil sales. It was daily commerce and agriculture—not petroleum—that powered the economy of the caliphate.[266]

At no point, however, does the Islamic State appear to have received direct state support. To be sure, it indirectly profited from state funding to the broader Syrian insurgency, including by skimming supplies intended for other rebel groups or purchasing weapons from those groups. The Islamic State also may have profited from quid pro quo exchanges and from extorting states, for example by holding hostages. Even so, the group appears to have been largely self-funded through taxation, oil and gas income, and institutional rents, helping to guarantee its independence in the face of state and nonstate enemies alike. However, although the longer-term economic sustainability of the Islamic State's state-building model appears dubious at best, it failed because of political and military opposition—and not because of flaws in the model itself. Islamic State governance simply could not survive the international onslaught triggered by the jihadists' aggressive, provocative policies and their gleeful broadcasting of videotaped atrocities.

Even though the Islamic State's governance project was conceptually at odds with the hybrid actor model, its dramatic rise and fall showcases the centrality of the state and stateness to the rise of hybrid actors and of other competitors to the state authority. Only in the context of a collapsing, distracted state could a group such as the Islamic State rise to such a scale, mounting an ambitious local challenge to the state system as such—and it could claim the administrative prowess of its caliphate only because it was able to incorporate existing state administrative institutions.

III. State Sponsorship

The use of proxies or nonstate allies is hardly unique to the Levant or the Middle East. In fact, during the Cold War the United States and the Soviet Union regularly used proxies as a means to limit the potential for superpower conflict and escalation, despite the serious costs imposed by proxy conflict. Traditionally, the logic underlying the use of proxies was clear in that it allowed patrons and sponsors to avoid "bearing the political, financial, and military burden of direct intervention."[267] In the present-day Middle East, the use of proxies and nonstate actors has been a practicable means for power projection and regional competition. This is particularly true for Iran, which has long-standing capacity in developing and sustaining partnerships with nonstate and militant actors. Iran also has been the most successful state in supporting and producing hybrid actors capable of influencing both their states and societies. Other states, including the United States, Israel, Turkey, Saudi Arabia, Qatar, and the United Arab Emirates, have invested considerably in proxies and hybrids. At the present historical juncture, however, none have done so as consistently and as effectively as Iran.

Iran has tempered the ideological motivations for its regional policy—it no longer seeks to export its revolution to the entire region—but it can still draw on its ideological ties with nonstate groups to create, cultivate, and sustain powerful substate actors. Iranian calculations as to when to intervene are most often governed by opportunity, in the form of conflict, degree of centrality to Iranian strategic goals, prospects for success, ease of access, and the nature of international ramifications. In this sense, Iran views Syria and Iraq much differently than it views, for example, Bahrain and Saudi Arabia. Indeed, Iran views Iraq as a first-order priority, and Syria as a key arena for its ability to grow its regional influence; by contrast, relations with nonstate actors in Saudi Arabia and Bahrain are useful only in that they allow Tehran to propagate its "defense of our Shia brothers" line and enable it to be a nuisance to Saudi Arabia, its regional rival.[268] This combination of pragmatic decision making coupled with ideological coherence once interventions are underway has proven successful in advancing Iranian influence, particularly in the current era of regional destabilization and conflict. But the practice of cultivating multiple competing power centers also comes with serious costs, and to date Iran has proven willing to bear them.

Iran's main rivals have experimented with a variety of different approaches. In some more recent cases of post–Arab uprisings such as Libya, Syria, and Yemen, Iran's rivals have engaged in revisionist intervention. For example, the United Arab Emirates' military intervention in Yemen might fit the same model of foreign sponsorship of hybrids. So might some historical cases, such as Israel's sponsorship of the Lebanese Forces. In other cases, Iran's rivals have upheld the status quo and tried to prop up existing states.

Tehran's success in the use of proxies is largely a function of structural advantages unavailable to Iran's key competitors and rivals. For various reasons, those states have not been able to recreate the conditions that allow for ideological, religious, political, and strategic convergence that typify Iran's most successful partnerships in the region. Though they are unlikely to be able to create convergence on all these issues, they may be able to achieve it on some. Those deficiencies have been on full display in recent years as those competitors, in the form of the Arab states of the Gulf, Turkey, and the United States, have all sought to cultivate nonstate partners, to decidedly mixed effect.

The Qualified Success of Iran

The Islamic Republic of Iran's reliance on proxies and nonstate actors was born out of its revolutionary ideology. After the 1979 revolution, through numerous speeches and writings, Supreme Leader Ayatollah Ruholla Khomeini established a duty to export Iran's Islamic revolution and to wage, by whatever means, a constant struggle against the perceived oppressor states. Today, the influence of Iran's revolutionary ideology over state policy has receded somewhat, as national interest and pragmatism have gradually taken over. But Tehran's reliance on these nonstate actors continues to fulfill a number of objectives. Iran uses proxies to pursue its interests, expand its regional influence, deter conventionally superior forces from attacking Iran, and deter foreign interference in the region, which it considers to be within its sphere of interest.[269] In distinction to its regional competitors, Iran's ability, in the words of analyst Afshon Ostovar, "to develop and sustain a clientage of allied co-religionist Shia militant organizations across the region" has enabled it to effectively project power throughout the region's conflict landscape.[270] Over the past few years of near-constant conflict intervention, Iran has made significant progress in improving its proxies' deployability, interoperability, and capacity to conduct unconventional warfare. It has moved beyond the revolutionary zeal that characterized its regional policy in the immediate aftermath of the Islamic revolution. But when it has chosen to project power—as a function of pragmatism, opportunism, or defensiveness—it has benefited from the ideological coherence that generally characterizes its interactions with its proxies and partners. In this sense, ideological ties, which encompass religious, political, and strategic views, have been a necessary but not sufficient condition for producing the most effective and sustainable patron-client relationships.

Analysts often perceive Iran's control over its proxies and partners as tight and total, but the reality is more nuanced than that.[271] Indeed, the degree of Iranian control over such groups is dependent on its interests in the area in which the group operates, its involvement in the group's creation, and Tehran's relationship with and trust in the group. For example, the degree of Iranian involvement in and control of Hezbollah's actions is different from that of the Houthis in Yemen. For that matter, control and influence over these groups are desirable, but some degree of deniability is also key: Tehran does not want to appear responsible for all actions these groups take, as that would diminish the groups' effectiveness for Tehran.

Iran's relationships with nonstate actors in the Middle East is a source of power and influence. But for others in the region and outside it, it is a nuisance. Countries in the region point to Tehran's relationship with nonstate actors as proof of its hegemonic ambitions and its desire to meddle in Arab affairs in order to destabilize the region. They attribute the prolonging of regional conflicts to Iran and the way it relies on nonstate groups. The Arab states of the Gulf regularly single out Tehran's relationship with its proxies as the cause of regional tensions, calling on the United States and its European allies to cease appeasing Tehran and address its regional ambitions.[272] "In Iraq and in Lebanon, the effects of regional interference are . . . stark," said Sheikh Khalid bin Ahmed Al Khalifa, Bahrain's minister of foreign affairs, in a 2018 speech. Iraq's and Lebanon's pursuit of prosperity, he added in a different address later that year, is impeded "by Iranian-backed groups or individuals who place loyalty to the Islamic Republic over the national interests of their countries, resulting in bad governance, inefficiency and ultimately political paralysis."[273] Al Khalifa also attributed the stalemate in Yemen to Iran's influence over the "terrorist" Houthis.[274] Similarly, in June 2019, the spokesperson for the Arab coalition fighting in Yemen attributed the worsening of the war to Iran's direct control of the Houthis, and their desire to control the Bab-el-Mandeb Strait.[275]

The Contingent Significance of Religious Identity

Iran's control of regional nonstate actors varies according to the group and the country it operates in, and the importance of the group's operating arena to Tehran. A proxy group's devotion to Iran's ruling principles also varies. Generally, when groups do not proclaim loyalty to the Islamic Republic's Rule of the Jurisprudent—the Shia principle that gives custodianship over the people to the "Islamic jurist" (a position filled by Iran's supreme leader)—it results in more limited Iranian control over their final decision making, giving greater weight to whether the proxy group itself wants closer ties with Tehran or not.[276]

Such religious ties, and a broader ideological and strategic affinity, have allowed Iran to cultivate enduring, disciplined relations with its closest partners and proxies. Other groups, such as the Houthis in Yemen, who are Zaydi Shia, present a different model of partnership. Though the Zaydis share similar worldviews and follow the same minority Muslim faith as Iran's leadership, they are a minority in the Shia community; their religious doctrine and beliefs are markedly different from the Shia in Iran, Iraq, and elsewhere in the region.[277] In fact, by some measures, Zaydi beliefs are actually more similar to Sunni Islam than Iranian Shiism.[278] In addition, the group's grievances are local and material, and hardly related to their religious beliefs: they are demanding equal access to political and civil rights and proportional representation, ending corruption, and curbing the spread of Salafism.[279]

As a result, the Houthis have maintained a degree of independence from Tehran, and wage war against the Yemeni government and the Saudi-led coalition irrespective of what Tehran wants. For example, according to U.S. intelligence, in 2015 Tehran ordered the Houthis not to enter Sana'a, in anticipation that this would lead to a conflict.[280] But the Houthis ignored Tehran's advice, leading to the beginning of the conflict with the Saudi-led coalition.[281] Even two years into the war in Yemen, the Quds Force of the Iranian Revolutionary Guard Corps (IRGC) reportedly tried to influence the Houthis into being more cooperative with Tehran and improving their targeting and strategy, to no avail.[282]

Thus, it is limiting to assess the relationship between Iran and its proxies and partners based solely on religious kinship and loyalty to the Rule of the Jurisprudent. According to the scholar Narges Bajoghli,

. . . what actually binds [Iranian proxy and partner] groups together is not an adherence to specific theological doctrine—if that were the case, Iran would not have close relationships with certain Palestinian factions, nor with Iraqi Kurdish groups, to say nothing of ties to Bashar al-Assad in Syria or the Houthis in Yemen. . . . When one pays close attention to the discourse of these groups, from their official statements to their media output, the emphasis is on sovereignty and the fight against imperialism. Of course the symbolism of Islam as a cultural and political identity is also present, but it is not the driving force.[283]

In other words, Iran's relationship with certain groups throughout the region is based in part on its image as a force battling imperialism and foreign interference in domestic affairs—a goal that Khomeini outlined in numerous speeches following the establishment of the Islamic Republic. This regional posture reflects another important dimension to Iran's ideological appeal that is distinct from its engagement with more doctrinaire coreligionist groups. Iran's 1979 revolution, while Islamic in nature, was also a struggle against the shah—a ruler the revolutionaries saw as an American puppet who did not have the interests of his nation at heart. In addition, Khomeini envisioned the Islamic Republic as the defender of minorities and the oppressed. Article 154 of the Islamic Republic's constitution states Iran's support for the "struggles of the oppressed for their rights against the oppressors." These views reflected the notion that "Iran and the Islamic world more broadly are in an existential conflict against Western imperialism," as Ostovar has put it.[284] This revisionist posture is distinctive and attractive to groups that are motivated to redraw the status quo, despite the potential costs of receiving patronage from Iran.[285] Nonetheless, such affinities toward Iran based on Iran's antagonistic regional posture are far more susceptible to changes in regional climate, as has been the case throughout the Arab uprisings and the ensuing period of conflict.[286]

Recent comments from Houthi leaders do, however, make clear that continued engagement can deepen bonds over time despite the lack of complete ideological convergence. The prolongation of the war in Yemen and the utility and effectiveness of Iran's relatively modest intervention have deepened relations between the Houthis and Iran. What began as a covert and deniable engagement has gradually grown into a recognized and public relationship. In a recent visit to meet with Iranian supreme leader Ayatollah Ali Khamenei, the Houthi envoy Mohammad Abdulsalam told Khamanei that "We consider your leadership to be the continuation of that of the prophet of Islam . . . and Imam Ali . . . and we consider your stance inspired by Imam Ali . . . in support of the oppressed people of Yemen in accordance with Imam Khomeini and a source of blessing and very heartwarming."[287] While stopping short of full-spectrum ideological commitment, the evocative religious rhetoric of the Houthi envoy reflects the way that religious ties, whether deeply or shallowly grounded in traditional doctrine, can be emphasized to strengthen relations. From the perspective of Iran, granting this form of public audience with the supreme leader is similar to the way in which it deals with its closest proxies.[288]

A comparable pattern can be discerned when examining the degree of control Tehran has over the followers of Muqtada al-Sadr in Iraq and Hamas in Palestine. Members of both groups have maintained a relationship with Tehran, yet Iranian investment in their movements has not translated into direct Iranian control over their actions and decision making. In these cases, by virtue of the provision of assistance and supplies, Tehran maintains a degree of influence over the groups, and advises them on policy decisions, but this does not mean they simply follow Tehran's orders.

Changeable Motivations for Sponsorship

Particularly with respect to its relationships with Sunni clients, Iran faces built-in limitations in terms of the depth, sustainability, and effectiveness of relations. In its approach to Palestinian militant groups, Iran has sought to emphasize the commonalities that flow from a commitment to political Islam and a commitment to anti-Israel regional politics.[289] Iran has thus been able to exploit its unique posture to forge ties with Sunni groups, particularly as these groups have only limited access to alternative sources of support. Prior to the deepening of sectarian polarization and conflict that began in the wake of the 2003 U.S.-led invasion of Iraq and that accelerated after the failed Arab uprisings that began in 2010, Iran's regional posture and positioning provided a pathway for forging ties and relations with Sunni Islamist groups in a few different countries in the region.

Iran initially welcomed the Arab uprisings of 2011, and Khamenei suggested that Iran's Islamic revolution was "a role model for these popular movements."[290] But as the nature of regional conflict has evolved, Iran's ability to exercise soft power and maintain its ties with such groups has suffered. In the intervening years, Iran has become a more sectarian actor, building deeper and more effective ties with Shia militant groups, while its links with Sunni actors have diminished. A particularly stark example of this dynamic can be seen in Iran's relationship with Hamas, a long-standing Iranian client that previously had housed much of its external senior leadership in Damascus. As the contours of the conflict in Syria evolved and took on an increasingly sectarian cast, Hamas chose to relocate its senior leadership and effectively broke with Iran. There are more recent signs of rapprochement, but the turbulent nature of the relationship is testament to the vulnerability of these types of cross-sectarian partnerships that lack full ideological convergence.

Iran's command and control over its proxies also depends on the level of trust it has in the group. For example, given Iran's involvement in the establishment of Hezbollah, the deep ties between Iran and the group, and the success of the movement, Hezbollah remains a fairly self-guided actor over whom Tehran has considerable influence. According to a Tehran-based Iranian academic, "the link between Iran and Hezbollah is very close. It takes two to three weeks for the cabinet to see the supreme leader, but Hassan Nasrallah will be granted an audience faster and with more ease than [Iranian president Has-san] Rouhani." The academic added that the situation is "the same" for Qasem Soleimani when the Quds Force leader seeks a meeting with Hezbollah's leadership.[291] But Tehran also recognizes that if Leb-anon is "going to be a nation state" then "Hezbollah can't be the only political player in town."[292] In other words, as this report has shown, Tehran allows Hezbollah considerable leeway in devising its political and policy priorities in Lebanon, the group's main area of operation.

The Popular Mobilization Units (PMU) in Iraq follows a similar pattern. Historically, Iran's relationship with Iraq's Shia communities has been tumultuous, as this report's case study on the PMU has shown.[293] Despite this tumultuous relationship, Iran works hard to maintain and expand ties with Iraq's Shias, considered a key con-stituency for Tehran. Iraq is, after all, a key area of interest for Iran, in which it has political, economic and religious interests it must secure. Tehran also remembers that the last time it was at odds with a strong Iraq, it faced eight years of devastating war.

In addition, much like the Houthis in Yemen, different Shia groups in Iraq also have their own interests, which at times are not in line with those of Tehran, making their loyalty to Tehran more fluid than Tehran would like.[294] Nevertheless, the long-standing political and religious kinship and ties between such groups and Tehran has given Iran a significant degree of influence over them—or at least among certain Shia factions in Iraq.[295] When Tehran trusts an organi-zation and its leaders, it welcomes their willingness to consider Ira-nian interests in their decision making, and can give them extensive leeway to conduct daily business in Iraq. This can be seen in the case of the Badr Organization, a PMU faction led by reliably pro-Iranian Hadi al-Amiri.[296] Amiri has continued to engage with U.S. diplomats in the country, despite his own ideological leanings and the escalat-ing tensions between the United States and Iran.[297] By contrast, the relative infancy of the nonstate actors that coordinate with Iran in Syria means they receive greater guidance from the IRGC in their decision making and actions.

Importantly, even if the actors in question are considered proxies of Tehran, if their interests diverge from those of Iran's, then it is
possible that they will not follow Tehran's advice or wishes because
the pursuit of their own interests generally remains the source of
their local power. Other groups have no choice but to accept Iranian
assistance, as was the case for Iran's outreach to the Shia Hazaras in
Afghanistan during the country's 1989–92 civil war, when anti-Shia
Afghan militants targeted that ethnic community. But according to
Iran expert Alex Vatanka, there "is a rich record of this community
resisting Iranian attempts to impose its ideological preferences on
them."[298] Many non-Shia groups that work with Tehran are reticent
to accept Iranian overlordship and have grown weary of its ideology.
In addition, in some cases there is value for the group in question to
demonstrate their relative independence from Tehran—knowing that
generally, the perception that the group merely follows the orders of
an external patron without consideration for the local cause or its
constituency will diminish its support base. In such cases, groups
will make their support to the Islamic Republic seem more grassroots
and voluntary, rather than one that is imposed from the top down.

For Tehran, the reliance on nonstate actors with local support
is a useful model, but their partial autonomy can be an additional
difficulty and a nuisance. This was the case with the outbreak of the
war in Yemen following the Houthis' takeover of Sana'a contrary to
Tehran's advice. The same can be said of Hamas's 2012 decision to
withdraw support for Bashar al-Assad in Syria—in direct opposition
to Iranian efforts.[299] It is challenging for Iran to manage the independence of its chosen nonstate actors, but the Islamic Republic's leadership considers it a natural result of its preferred model and continues
to work with the relationships as best it can.[300]

The Magnitude of Iran's Support

The extent of Iran's assistance to foreign militias and nonstate actors
in the region has been the cause of much debate. There is little
consensus on the magnitude of aid. The United States estimates

that Iran spends about $1 billion a year on proxies in the region; other estimates have suggested Iran spends $15–20 billion in Syria alone.[301] Generally, Tehran's assistance is deliberately opaque and nontraceable, varying widely according to the importance to Iran of the group in question. Conversely, overt transfers of assistance are deliberately designed to be grand political statements of support for the group in question.

Tehran has devoted significant sums of money to maintaining the links it has with nonstate actors in the region—and this despite the internal economic difficulties it faces. One of the leading criticisms of the 2015 nuclear deal with Iran was that it supposedly provided a cash windfall that Iran would pour into its nefarious activities in the region.[302] But Tehran's regional operations have been relatively stable despite its economic troubles and the sanctions: it continued its support to regional proxies even when faced with the most draconian sanctions following 2010, and again, following the reimposition of sanctions under U.S. president Donald Trump.[303]

One of the reasons that Tehran is able to maintain a steady stream of support for these groups despite internal economic difficulties is that it does not draw the money it uses to fund its chosen groups from budgets that are under public scrutiny. The majority of the funding comes from significant sums that are under the direct control of the supreme leader's office and the IRGC, and hidden from public view, as explained below.

The IRGC

After the 1979 revolution, the emerging Islamic Republic needed to consolidate its power. This involved carrying out two significant measures. First, the leader of the revolution, Khomeini, preached the spread of the revolution outside Iran.[304] In fact, it committed, in the words of Vatanka, "to a mission of mobilizing the mostazafeen, so-called downtrodden Muslims, against what Tehran labelled unjust rulers. This refers to Muslims in general and did not distinguish between Shi'a and Sunnis."[305] To that end, Tehran began to create or establish ties with various nonstate actors and minority groups in the region, including Hezbollah in Lebanon and the Badr Brigades in Iraq. The second measure was the implementation of military purges to eradicate those who might harbor sympathies for the deposed shah and ensure the loyalties of remaining personnel; coupled with the devastating eight-year Iran-Iraq War, this culling of the ranks greatly weakened the Iranian military.[306] To ensure the security of the regime and the revolution, the Islamic Republic created organizations, such as the IRGC, that were intended to operate both within Iran and outside its borders. Today, many key security files are either directly held by the IRGC or shared between the IRGC and the government and its Ministry of Foreign Affairs. Iran's management of its relations with nonstate actors in the region is largely within the mandate of the IRGC, making it a powerful actor in Iran's foreign relations.

Following the 1979 revolution, Iran's military was split because its loyalty to the revolution was questioned by those who had just come to power. Iran's traditional military, known in Persian as the Artesh, had been established in its modern form by Iran's previous ruler, Reza Shah. The revolutionaries viewed it with extreme suspicion; under the shah, the army had collaborated with the United States, a key enemy of the revolution. As a result, the Islamic Republic established the IRGC as a paramilitary organization, and charged it with providing a counterweight to the traditional military and spreading the values of the revolution inside and outside Iran.[307]

Today, the IRGC has expanded to include members and former members in all spheres of life in Iran, from the parliament), to ministries, and including the national security council. Though estimates vary widely, it is thought that the Guards count between 120,000 and 300,000 members. However, the IRGC's notorious plainclothes militia, the Basij, can mobilize up to an additional 600,000 people.[308] Since the revolution, the IRGC has grown in number and importance. Today, it operates under the supervision of the supreme leader and conducts overt and covert operations at home and abroad. It is professional and voluntary; has air, sea, and land components; and oversees key Iranian military programs, including its ballistic missile, nuclear, space, and drone programs, and Iran's cyber activities. The IRGC's navy, for example, is separate from Iran's national navy, and is tasked with patrolling the country's maritime borders, including the Strait of Hormuz, through which a large portion of the world's oil is shipped. The IRGC is composed of several branches, including two organizations known for their counterintelligence and covert operations in the region and beyond: the Ansar al-Mahdi and the Quds Force. The IRGC owes part of its strength to its solid relationship with the supreme leader and his office, which Iran analyst Karim Sadjadpour describes as "increasingly symbiotic, politically expedient for the Leader and economically expedient for the guards." The supreme leader is the commander in chief of the IRGC and "appoints [its] senior commanders, who, in turn, are publicly deferential to him and increasingly reap benefits by playing a more active role in political decision making and economic activity."[309] But while it is known that the IRGC has strong ties to the supreme leader, their precise nature is relatively opaque, as are the Guards' internal dynamics and its ties with the rest of the political establishment.

The IRGC is a real economic and political powerhouse in Iran, controlling billions of dollars' worth of projects. The Guards have stakes in many industries, especially infrastructure, telecommunications, and the energy sector. Their influence over the economy grew with subsequent waves of sanctions. Today, they control a substantial portion of Iran's economy—estimates of exactly how much vary widely, from a little less than a third to two-thirds.[310] What is undeniable is that the IRGC is involved in almost every key sector in the Iranian economy, and continues to enrich itself through the significant shadow economy. Both the office of the supreme leader and the IRGC have developed their income as a result of vast business networks, which have *gained* in strength and size following the imposition of multiple rounds of sanctions on Iran.[311] Indeed, as sanctions made it more difficult to maintain business links to Iran, small and medium-sized Iranian businesses could not continue to operate in an environment of ever-increasing costs and significant barriers to trade. The only organizations with the ability to overcome the costs of business were giant conglomerations directly owned by or with significant ties to either the IRGC or the supreme leader's office. As a result, contrary to what the calls to squeeze Iran's elite aimed to achieve, the sanctions further strengthened the hold of the elite in the Iranian economy. Most notably, they strengthened the IRGC, and provided it with the means to continue its involvement in the region, including its support to regional nonstate actors.[312]

The IRGC's influence on foreign policy and security policy grew as its size and finances did, and as the opportunities for intervention proliferated across the region. Since the 2009 elections and the failed Green Movement that contested their results, IRGC control over the domestic sphere has grown further, as its forces attempted to secure the Islamic Republic, at times even undermining the work of the Ministry of Intelligence. Most of the regional security files, including Iran's work with and influence over regional proxies and nonstate actors, fall within the remit of the IRGC.[313]

Iraq, for example, is a key arena for Iran, particularly since 2003. Iraq and Iran have been enemies, rivals, or strategic partners at various points in history; have religious, economic and political ties; and share more than nine hundred miles of porous border.[314] Iran's foreign policy for its western neighbor has been the cause of internal bickering between the IRGC and the Ministry of Foreign Affairs, as the latter tried to regain greater influence. The work of setting regional policy and coordinating with Iranian regional nonstate allies falls to the IRGC's elite unit, the Quds Force. The Quds Force mandate extends specifically beyond Iran's borders, initially intending to export the revolution. Today, Quds Force commander Qasem Soleimani answers only to the supreme leader, though he continues to hold frequent meetings with different parts of the government.

As the head of the Quds Force, Soleimani holds direct influence over Iran's relations with regional nonstate actors. He has been developing personal relations with the leadership and membership of key groups in the region—activities that Tehran has often advertised. In 2014, Iran launched a public relations campaign aimed at both domestic and foreign audiences. This campaign was designed to burnish Iran's image, which had been harmed by the 2009 protest movement, and to highlight its actions against the rise of the Islamic State in Iraq and Syria.[315] The campaign highlighted Soleimani's good personal relations with key figures in the region, beginning with the Badr Organization and peshmerga commanders.[316] At the same time, it aimed to showcase the IRGC commander's relations with multiple tribes and different religious and ethnic groups, in the hopes of reducing perceptions that Tehran was solely a sectarian actor.[317] The campaign presented the IRGC as helping the homeland, giving it newfound popularity and legitimacy within Iran. But with greater popularity and awareness of the actions of the IRGC came greater public scrutiny, including the beginning of a campaign launched by Rouhani to contain their influence.[318]

Iraq has been a laboratory for IRGC experimentation, and an example of the success for its model of establishing relationships with and control over local nonstate actors. During Saddam Hussein's rule, many key Shia figures took asylum in Iran.[319] As a result, 2003 invasion upended the regional order, and created in Iraq a political void and an opportunity for Tehran. The IRGC benefited from its long-standing ties to Iraqi expatriate groups, such as the Supreme Council for Islamic Revolution in Iraq, which had been founded by pro-Khomeini Shia activists in Iran during the 1980s, and the council's military wing, the Badr Brigades (today's Badr Organization). In the years following the 2003 invasion, members of these groups and others friendly with Iran began to occupy influential positions in Iraq's political and military establishments, effectively expanding the reach and influence of the IRGC. The Guards also promoted the development of a new cadre of more extreme and more outwardly pro-Iranian allies among Iraq's Shia militants; these were drawn upon to target and harass U.S. forces in the country.

The Islamic State takeover of large swathes of Iraqi territory in 2014 was a major concern to Iran, especially when the group came close to the Iranian border. It developed a strategy to counter the Islamic State in Iraq by relying on local forces, which it assisted economically, politically and militarily. In this way, it organized its interests under the umbrella of the PMU. Iran also drew on local actors beyond just the Shia militias, which helped delegitimize and undermine the Islamic State. After initial hesitation, Iran supported the Baghdad government and various Kurdish, Shia, and Sunni groups' efforts against the Islamic State.[320] Tehran's efforts were successful in part because Soleimani had long maintained good relations with a diverse roster of groups and important individuals in Iraq—including Sunnis, Kurds, and Shia—and had been involved in key deliberations within the Iraqi government since 2003.[321] Historical and cultural ties also bolstered Iran's coordination with Iraq's Sunni-majority Kurds.[322] Iranian attempts at working with Arab Sunnis in Iraq were less successful. Marginalized Sunnis had grown wary of Tehran and its support for the Shia government, and Iran managed to recruit only a few hundred Sunni fighters.[323]

In the fight against the Islamic State, Iran provided a range of assistance to myriad actors in the region. Importantly, despite its initial strategy of leading the campaign by relying on local forces, it sent IRGC commanders to oversee and lead the militias it worked with, and even committed Iranian combat troops. It also provided indirect assistance through its backing of Lebanese Hezbollah, which was supporting the fight against the Islamic State.[324]

Yet Tehran's strategy to fight the Islamic State had certain inconsistencies that underline the way in which Iran pursues different tracks simultaneously in pursuit of major objectives. For instance, Tehran also coordinated ground operations with the U.S. forces that were conducting airstrikes to drive back the Islamic State. The Rouhani administration led this push to coordinate with Washington. At the same time, and despite its overtures to non-Shia groups, IRGC-led Shia militias further exacerbated sectarian divisions in the country, including by persecuting Sunnis, flying Shia flags, and plastering pictures of Iranian religious leaders in recaptured territories.[325]

Changing War Strategies

Though Iran's model of increasing its regional influence through the use of local nonstate actors throughout the region has been relatively consistent, the way it draws on these actors has evolved. In Syria, for example, Iran brought in advisors to help the Assad government conduct its campaign after conflict broke out in 2011. Iran also drew on local militias as foot soldiers for the government's air campaign, providing assistance and advice to pro-Assad fighters. Iran also coordinated its efforts with the Russians once they joined the fight, allowing Tehran to learn from them. Iran is reported to have deployed 10,000 personnel to Syria from 2011 to 2014, including combat troops, and to have suffered 2,100 dead by 2017.[326]

In addition, Tehran has leveraged new, militant Shia clergy throughout the region (as well as domestically) to boost their power. This allows them to have greater fighting numbers and a more significant impact in battle. For example, Tehran drew on the Fatemiyoun Brigade, an Afghan Shia militia allied with Bashar al-Assad, whose members are Afghan seminary graduates of Al-Mustafa International University in Qom, Iran. Originally a small group of volunteers and refugees tasked with defending the shrine of Saida Zaynab near Damascus, the brigade has grown in number and strength.[327] But this was not the only group of foreigners Tehran was drawing on in its fight in Syria. Following a rocket attack on the Saida Zaynab shrine in 2013, Shia Pakistani jihadists formed the Zaynabiyoun Brigade with support from Tehran, and the brigade recruited Pakistani Shia seminary students studying in Iran.[328] Tehran also relies on Iraqi Shia militias in Syria, which include several militant clergy members, though they seemed to have only conducted operations jointly with other groups in Syria, likely because the majority of Iraqi Shia fighters were involved in combating the Islamic State in Iraq.[329]

The IRGC's use of these groups has helped Tehran contribute to turning the tide of war in Syria in favor of the Assad government. Tehran seems to want to keep these groups as separate brigades in Syria, rather than unifying them under an umbrella organization as they were in Iraq. Naturally, Tehran does not want them to become too powerful—it would be better if they remain dependent on Iran. It seems likely that Tehran continues to draw lessons from its model of relying on local nonstate actors in regional warfare and policymaking, and adapting its approach according to the particular context on the ground. But drawing on this new wave of Shia militancy will further politicize and radicalize Shia authority, as the Shia clergy militias gain influence throughout the region.

In the past few years, Tehran has made serious progress in effectively deploying its proxies in the region, in its capacity to conduct unconventional warfare successfully as a result of these deployments, and in its proxies' interoperability. As a result, despite serious constraints ranging from successive waves of sanctions, to international political and even military pressure today, the IRGC has continued to be involved in the region, strengthened its influence throughout the Middle East, maintained pressure on U.S. forces deployed in the region, and successfully increased its popularity in Iran and the sense of nationalism surrounding them by portraying themselves as defenders of Iranian territorial integrity, particularly following the rise of the Islamic State in neighboring Iraq. But the IRGC has not succeeded on every level. Its reliance on overly sectarian groups, particularly in Iraq, has turned some local populations against it, increasing resentment of Iranian presence.[330] In addition, the IRGC's public relations campaign, whatever popularity it may have gained the corps, also means that the Guards are now under greater public scrutiny.

The IRGC largely succeeded in implementing its model of working with nonstate actors to increase Iran's influence in the region despite continued internationally enforced pressure and efforts to contain Iran. But it remains to be seen whether this strategy will continue to yield the same level of success. Much depends on the Guards' standing among the groups they support in the Arab world (and among those groups' constituencies) and their popularity at home.[331]

Regional Competition

The use or support of nonstate actors, including hybrids, is hardly unique to Iran. Other regional states and key international players, like the United States, have sought to accomplish political and military goals in this manner, particularly in the kind of open-ended conflict that has proliferated in the Arab world following the serial failure of the uprisings that began in late 2010. Nonetheless, those other countries' experiences have highlighted the structural advantages Iran enjoys in this domain, and it is highly unlikely that other states will enjoy the same sort of success that Iran has achieved. At the same time, other comparisons reveal that, when Iran's structural advantages are not as strong, the results of its partnerships with nonstate actors are more checkered.

Foremost among Iranian structural advantages is the ideological cohesion between patron and client. This is a reflection of the fact that, as Ostovar writes, "supporting foreign militants has been central to the Islamic Republic's grand strategy since its establishment."[332] Shia militancy grew and developed in lockstep with the revolutionary vision of the early Islamic Republic, coming out of Tehran's ideological framework and later sustained under its tutelage. In comparison, Sunni militancy arose in opposition to the Arab republics and, in later years, to the monarchies of the region. This fundamental difference ensures that the efforts of other regional and international states to cultivate nonstate allies and partners almost certainly are based on thinner ideological connectivity and weaker bonds of trust, and are much more volatile with respect to unintended consequences. As a vanguard actor, Iran has credibility with its militant clients that cannot be easily replicated. Whereas the Sunni states of the region are often themselves the targets of militant actors, Iran's strategic vision is more aligned with the outer spectrum of Shia militancy.

That posture is further enhanced by Iran's revisionist stances, which highlight key differences with its competitors and rivals. Iran's closest nonstate allies share its regional orientation and its core antagonisms. Central to that worldview is hostility to the United States, Israel, and foreign involvement in the region. The closeness in perspective of these allies has created much greater opportunities for sustainable coordination, as Iran's strategic orientation has remained fairly constant despite the tempering of its initial revolutionary fervor. In contrast, Iran's regional competitors and rivals are all part of the United States' regional security architecture. As U.S. clients and allies, the key Sunni Arab states and Turkey relate differently to nonstate actors, in particular those of the militant variety. Iran remains embedded within the structures of Shia militancy and has not been outflanked by its clients or other state sponsors.

In this sense, Iran remains overtly committed to militancy—notwithstanding its parallel commitment to pragmatism—in a manner that is not open to its regional competitors, despite instances in which those states have engaged with militants and sanctioned groups. The ongoing civil war in Syria illustrates this phenomenon. First, there is no credible evidence to suggest the existence of overt state support and funding for the Islamic State—the most violent and ideologically extreme Sunni actor in the conflict. However, there is considerable evidence for passive forms of support for the Islamic State, such as lax and irresponsible Turkish border control.[333] Although Turkey's passivity at the border fell short of actively providing sanctuary for the Islamic State, the group benefited from Turkey's neglect for a number of years. Similarly, hardline Islamist factions benefited from private fundraising and charitable giving from the Gulf, which could not have operated without an environment of lax enforcement.[334] But the Sunni states involved in the war in Syria have not, for a variety of reasons, contemplated direct support for the outer boundaries of Sunni militancy. This reticence reflects their reputational concerns, their alliance and partnership structures, their relative inexperience in engaging in this manner, and their concerns over the longer-term ramifications of such endeavors—particularly with respect to unintended consequences and potential blowback.

Even when states have offered support to Sunni rebel groups and armed actors in the Syrian war, assistance has been offered with unease and difficulty. In an effort to attract outside support and patronage, various hardline Islamist groups have, at several junctures, sought to differentiate themselves from more problematic actors, such as the Nusra Front.[335] Ahrar al-Sham, which enjoyed productive battlefield relations with the Nusra Front and lauded the latter's warfighting contributions, still sought to contrast itself with Nusra in an effort to legitimize the group and to allow for the possibility of outside assistance.[336]

Western governments and their allies in the region have a demonstrated track record of refusing to deal directly with a subset of extremist groups, even when those groups are willing to work in concert with Western interests. This self-imposed limitation usually takes the form of terror designations or sanctions against groups with extremist ideology or especially violent tactics. In Syria, the United States and its allies allowed designated or proscribed militant groups to benefit indirectly from Western aid but withheld direct assistance. In contrast, Iran is willing to work with virtually any armed group that will accept Iranian assistance and serve a minimal Iranian interest—even in limited circumstances sectarian Salafi-jihadist groups that are ideologically opposed to Iran's policies and the very existence of Shia Muslims. This flexibility distinguishes Iran's approach to hybrids from that of many of its competitor states.

There is also a fundamental difference in the ways in which Iran and its competitors function within the international system. First, Iran's regional posture and worldview have placed it at odds with much of the Middle East and North Africa. To compensate for its lack of natural allies, writes Ostovar, "Iran's revolutionary leaders sought to develop allies at the substate level."[337] Second, the strategic benefits afforded Iran through these relationships and Iran's ideological convergence with its clients have all combined to ensure continued Iranian support for these groups, despite the reputational and legal exposure those ties create. Iran continues to display a willing-ness to endure the international costs and reputational damage. In contrast, Iran's competitors are unable to provide this type of direct, overt support for formally designated terrorist groups. Most foreign interventionist powers prefer a close relationship with a state to a closer relationship with a hybrid or proxy, when such a partnership is on offer. Iran cannot be said to have total control over its partners, but it does not run the same types of risks faced by other states, where there is either limited or no strategic alignment. In the case of regional Sunni powers with an investment in the status quo, it comes as little surprise that their engagements with revisionist mil-itants have been fraught, since the Arab state system itself is often a key target for Sunni Islamist extremists.

Still, this does not mean that Iran exclusively partners with non-state actors, nor that other countries completely eschew them. Iran's choice about whom to support, and how, greatly depends on local priorities. In Iraq, for instance, Iran cultivates ties with hybrids and proxies, but also invests in its partnership with the national and local governments. In Syria, Iran valued its partnership with the president over its investment in the National Defence Forces, helping estab-lish it as a pseudogovernmental entity instead of driving toward full-blown hybrid status. The United States and regional governments sometimes rely on proxies and hybrids for military operations or for political moves that are considered risky or unpalatable, or require plausible deniability for their sponsors. Iran's ideology affords it unique opportunities as it cultivates partnerships. As a result of the greater convergence of ideology and interests among Iran and its allies, it has been much better placed in managing the impact of this type of engagement with armed proxies and militant groups.

Beyond the Middle East, Pakistan provides an instructive con-trasting example of contemporary state sponsorship of militancy. Pakistan has been more successful than Iran in weathering the inter-national opprobrium and fallout that has resulted from its policies with respect to militant groups such as Lashkar-e-Taiba and the

Afghan Taliban. However, even though Pakistani strategic planners believe their support for militants has been successful both in its asymmetric competition with India and in the protection of what they have deemed to be their strategic depth in Afghanistan, they have been unable to fully control the effects of militancy on their society and state. The unintended consequences of that support have produced their own forms of domestic blowback and insurgency. Iran, by contrast, has not suffered in the same manner.

Iran's unique experience is also a function of the country's distinct position as one of the few Shia-majority states, and perhaps the only option, that Shia militant groups have when seeking international support. Functionally, there are no alternatives for nonstate Shia actors, and, in some cases, none for Sunni militant groups, either.

As a revisionist power, in certain instances Iran's goals have been framed negatively in terms of thwarting the goals and undermining the interests of the United States and its regional partners. In those instances, playing the spoiler—as opposed to pursuing more ambitious political goals—offers Iran varied points of entry into certain regional conflicts.

Lastly, and crucially, Iran enjoys an advantage because it has been engaged in the cultivation and support of nonstate groups for decades, and those efforts have only accelerated over time. Beginning with its immediate postrevolutionary efforts to cultivate militant allies, Iran has had continuous, uninterrupted engagement with militant partners. In more recent years, two major regional disruptions created significant strategic openings that have aided Iran's efforts. First, the 2003 invasion of Iraq eliminated a key Iranian rival and security vulnerability, while providing Iran with a major political and military opportunity. The institution of electoral politics in a Shia-majority state also ensured, for the foreseeable future, a Shia-led political order and friendly relations between Iran and Iraq. Second, the failed Arab uprisings that began in 2010 initiated a tumultuous period of conflict ripe for Iranian intervention. Syria in particular, with its long-standing alliance with Iran and its strategic centrality to its regional policy, was an obvious national security interest for the Iranian leadership. Syria's relative importance and the early setbacks suffered by the Assad regime not only necessitated Iranian support for various nonstate groups but also, as noted above, triggered direct Iranian intervention. This novel form of direct intervention is further testament to the practical experience and capacity built up through its recent interventions. Iran's careful selections of the specific areas and conflicts in which it has intervened have allowed it to benefit from the existence of natural allies and assured access.

On the whole, these interventions have produced tangible gains for Iran, and yet they have come with serious costs, including the withering of Iranian soft power in much of the Arab world and the sectarianization of its power projection. This latter point has been a particularly large sacrifice for Iran, as its ability to sustain its relationships with Sunni militant partners has suffered. These dysfunctional patron-client relationships in which Iran does not enjoy ideological, religious, strategic, and political convergence with its militant clients offer a useful point of comparison with the similarly checkered record of its Sunni rivals. In spite of various Sunni regimes' transactional dalliances and engagements with Sunni militants, the two groups have never overcome their fundamental divergence in end-state political aims. Likewise, Iran's efforts at engaging Sunni militants have been undermined by a similar lack of connectivity and overlap. Stresses resulting from Iran's sectarian mobilization have exposed these gaps. In this sense, cases in which Iran has not been afforded the full benefit of its structural advantages help to illuminate the sources of its success. In those instances in which Iran is capable of engaging in only a more transactional and limited capacity, as with its engagement with Sunni militants such as the Taliban, al-Qaeda, and Hezb-e-Islami, it displays much less control over its partners and has produced more inconclusive results.[338] Even in instances in which Iran has engaged with more ideologically aligned Sunni groups, such as Hamas, those relationships have proven less durable and have not grown into a full-spectrum alliance.

IV. Policy Implications

Hybrid actors differ from traditional proxies and other militias because of their complex relationships with states. Hybrids draw some of their power from states, and at the same time, in many contexts hybrids compete directly with the state. Hybrids can function as a Trojan horse for interventionist foreign powers; at times, and even sometimes simultaneously, they can operate independently of those sponsors. They figure as a significant and standing addition to the landscape of power. Any coherent policy response depends on a clear understanding of hybrids: armed groups that can operate in concert with the state, in parallel to it, and in competition with it.

Policy that aims to promote security and good governance ought to take into account the special constraints and challenges hybrid actors pose. Policymakers cannot simply ignore the existence of hybrids, dealing only with their sponsor or host states. Hybrids matter because of their state relations, their coercive power, and their constituencies. An effective policy must account for them as centers of power and decision making in conflict zones where significant interests are at stake.

Promoting Rule of Law

Security and accountability benefit when major power players are embedded in a legal framework that revolves around the state, and in which both hybrid actors and the central government are subject to the same rule of law. In conflict zones with eroded central authority, policymakers should not seek solutions that are impractically idealistic. For example, Iraq will not quickly develop a single cohesive, credible, and just national authority with rule of law. But it can consolidate law and authority under the umbrella of the state, in a manner that incrementally promotes norms and values consistent with Iraqi preferences, Iraqi law, and the conventions of international treaties and institutions to which Iraq is a party.

Our study of hybrids, and the new concepts that we have developed, suggest an array of approaches for policymakers, including the following:

- Engage with hybrid actors and incorporate them, even incrementally, into state, multilateral, and international institutions.
- Use policy tools to encourage sponsors of hybrid actors to modulate their influence over hybrids.
- Constrain hybrid actors by strengthening host states and security institutions that are broader and more domestically legitimate than the hybrid's militia.
- Consider incorporating hybrids—even those that are destabilizing—into functioning states as a suboptimal but practical path to stability and accountability, intended to improve the behavior of both the state and the hybrid.

Hybrid actors today pose one of the most significant obstacles to consolidating state authority. Realistic solutions cannot be based on an unfounded hope that troublesome or powerful hybrids will simply disappear. Hybrids cannot be wished away. Other types of groups, such as classic nonstate proxies or aspirants to full statehood, merit different analytical and policy treatment than hybrids.

States in Conflict

An honest reckoning with hybrid actors connects directly to our understanding of the eroded power of the state. Fundamentally, the success of nonstate actors has been dependent on conflict, the erosion of governmental authority, and the resulting weakness of states. As with the most militant actors, conflict presents opportunities for nonstate groups. This is perhaps self-evident, but it is indisputably true that "wars, state collapse, and geopolitical upheaval" have provided and will continue to provide a fertile backdrop for these opportunities.[339] Those opportunities have been furthered by the deepening and accelerating nature of regional competition and the more frequent resort by influential regional and international players to employing nonstate allies to achieve policy ends.

The strongest hybrid actors arise in the vacuums created by weak and fragile states and eventually become the greatest challenge to the strengthening of state sovereignty. The greatest opportunity for nonstate groups is presented by those states and societies that have been fundamentally altered by open-ended, multiyear conflict. Although Iraq traditionally had been accustomed to strong centralized governance and repression, the period before the U.S. invasion of Iraq in 2003 had seen Saddam Hussein's regime systematically degraded through a cycle of war and sanctions. When coupled with the prolonged period of chaos and conflict that followed the overthrow of the Ba'athist regime, Iraq experienced a multidecade process of institutional decay and a retreat of the central state. In such conditions, it is unsurprising that nonstate and hybrid actors have been able to flourish. The example of the Syrian NDF offers an alternative example of a weakened state that still sought to exercise strong centralized authority and remained capable of managing nonstate actors within the areas under its control. This more limited vacuum, while damaging to the regime, did not cripple its ability to project its practical and symbolic centrality. A longer-term lack of control over territory, such as Idlib governorate and the Syrian Democratic Forces-held portions of northeastern Syria, will create greater challenges for the reassertion of centrality while creating practical opportunities for nonstate groups in those areas to develop hybrid characteristics. Prolonged conflict conditions and more extended gaps in governmental authority produce outcomes much more favorable to nonstate actors.

These negative trends have been strengthened by the failures of the international community at conflict prevention and mitigation and postconflict stabilization and reconstruction. Such failures have created real dangers to international peace and security. There is no easy answer to these dilemmas, particularly at a time of increased international economic uncertainty, rising populist politics, accelerating climate change, great power competition, and diminished collective security. The need to reverse these trends is as acute as the gaps in capacity to do so.

The necessity for strong and functional states is clear, but the legacy of such states in the region is checkered at best. Strong states, such as Saddam Hussein's Iraq or Syria under the Assads, have been most successful in producing brittle stability through repression and fear. The harm that strong states have inflicted on their own people and rival powers has created lasting legacies, among which is suspicion of strong centralized authority among victimized segments of society. Those suspicions are understandable, yet have produced their own institutional legacies that undermine the ability to produce effective governance.

Even in instances where states and governments are intent on producing gains in governance, the challenges resulting from decades-long dysfunction and misrule remain steep. The overall landscape is grim and the ability to induce sustainable positive change is limited. As such, the issues of nonstate and hybrid actors and how best to respond to them on both the domestic and international levels remain central to the future of the region and a key determinant of regional peace and security.

Partition Is Not the Answer

New realities on the ground, in the form of powerful and sustainable hybrid actors, are now a fundamental feature of the region and must be addressed. As a practical matter, it is unlikely that hybrid or quasi-state actors will receive de jure recognition as new states. With the notable exception of the secession of South Sudan in 2011, the international climate has been nearly universally hostile to recognizing and formalizing state fragmentation in postcolonial areas, including in the Middle East. Hybrid actors and quasi-states are therefore unlikely to produce a formal redrawing of the regional state system. Fears of negative precedent and destabilizing cascade effects in this tense, unstable area have created deep-rooted caution with respect to secessionist movements and the prospect of new state formation. This means that the traditional boundaries of the regional order will continue to frame the ways in which host states and outside actors engage with hybrid groups.

As in the recent past, these realities are likely to mean that there will be further attempts to confer formal recognition on certain actors as legitimate but still nonstate entities, either through ambiguous bilateral relationships or by promoting federalism and similar concepts as a way to legalize such groups within a preserved state framework. This can be seen in the constitutional treatment of the Kurdistan Regional Government and the asymmetric federalism that typifies the Iraqi constitutional order. The legacies of colonialism have created enduring suspicions about such efforts, and citizens in the region have regarded any attempts at creating decentralized models of governance, whether by national governments or by foreign powers, as a prelude to partition. Nonetheless, they continue to offer one pathway for enhancing autonomy without full de jure recognition of separatism. These kinds of arrangements could have particular salience for the future prospects for Kurdish self-rule in Syria and South Yemeni separatism. On the less statelike end, the region also has seen direct diplomatic engagement with powerful hybrid actors, such as Hezbollah. This type of engagement remains fraught and difficult to balance with support for regional states, but simply choosing to ignore hybrid actors that have emerged as effective political and security actors will neither diminish their relevance nor strengthen the central state. Further, the most effective hybrid actors have enmeshed themselves within their host states and, as such, have formalized their presence within various levels of government.

For outside actors seeking to strengthen state structures and limit the negative impact of nonstate actors, it is critical to differentiate among hybrid actors and proxy groups. As Michael Knights argues in the context of Iraq, "Many average citizens have relatives who fought honorably in the [Popular Mobilization Units] structure primarily for the benefit of Iraq, not Iran or pro-Iranian militia leaders. The U.S. government arguably alienates potential allies when it publicly criticizes the [PMU] phenomenon in a generalized manner."[340] Further, in the case of Iraq, there are also relevant distinctions to be made between full-fledged proxies of Iran, as opposed to other elements of the PMU that are more rightly understood as Iranian allies and partners. Such distinctions matter a great deal in terms of explaining the motivations of nonstate groups and predicting future behavior.

In determining how to engage with hybrid actors, outside actors must be cognizant that they are rarely in a position to pick winners.[341] Outside intervention and support for certain groups can help shape the role of nonstate groups, but efforts at "integrating unfavoured actors into unpopular political settlements" are likely to be ineffective and potentially destabilizing.[342] This is not to suggest passivity. Outside actors should instead incentivize "a process of bargaining and integration that rewards cooperation, and that applies punitive measures where actors violate the rule of law and/or cause harm to society."[343] Western governments have frequently resorted to terror designations to sanction individual militants and sometimes entire groups or entities. The European Union has often followed the lead of the United States, the United Kingdom, and France in designating groups. The international community has been more circumspect; United Nations sanctions, for instance, have been applied to the Taliban, al-Qaeda, and the Islamic State. Terror designations are inherently political, since they do not extend universally to all groups that engage in illegal violence targeting civilians. Their utility has also been subject to debate; even the United States, which is the most vocal advocate of bans and terror designations, has engaged in indirect contact with proscribed groups or allowed indirect aid to flow to them. Yet at the same time, proscription has served as an effective sanction against groups, at a minimum making it harder for them to operate internationally or receive overt political and military support. Designation has been more effective against individuals than entire groups.

The desire of hybrid actors, in contrast to classic proxies, for recognition and legitimacy offers a useful avenue for pressure and incremental change. Governments interested in steering the course of hybrids or integrating them into the state will need to engage directly with those hybrid groups. Bans and terror lists, however, make such contacts difficult. Even aid workers and low-level officials from the military, diplomatic corps, and intelligence services might consider themselves legally barred by their own governments from even the most minimal communications with members of designated groups. A further complication is that governments historically have found it much harder to remove groups from terror lists than to designate them. Bans on engagement create a dilemma for policymakers who seek to change the behavior of proscribed groups but find themselves unable to gather information or explore potential solutions.

The case studies in this report offer some suggestions for ways forward. For example, in Iraq, the largely autonomous militias of the PMU have, in a period of a few years, been formally integrated under state authority. The legal framework that normalized the PMU is profoundly flawed, and reflects the weakness of the state that negotiated it with Iraq's hybrids and their sponsors. The years to come will show whether the state is able to translate its nominal legal powers over the PMU into genuine authority, but the Iraqi approach suggests one policy framework for integrating hybrids more closely into the state. The Syrian government's thus far sustained authority over the NDF and other loyalist militias is another ambiguous example of a state consolidating authority by both institutional and informal means. Lebanon's Hezbollah provides a third, cautionary example:

in a context where domestic power centers and foreign governments refuse to engage with a significant hybrid—and crucially, refrain from investing seriously in state power as an alternative to a hybrid—the hybrid can become as strong as the state, or at least, too strong to subordinate.

Dealing with State Sponsors

The depth and breadth of hybrid actor activity, particularly of Iranian-backed groups, suggests that this set of challenges will remain for the foreseeable future. In initiating analysis and formulating policy responses, it should be clear that while Iran has structural advantages in supporting or creating nonstate and hybrid groups, it does not have magical powers. When Iran's structural advantages are weaker, its partnerships with nonstate actors have produced more limited and mixed results. However, in those instances where structural factors align, it is difficult for outside actors to either frustrate or break such bonds. Nonetheless, those cases of maximal alignment, such as with Hezbollah or the PMU, are unique, and should not be conflated with other partners, such as the Houthis, who have productive and increasing relations with Iran but do not represent the most optimal version of alignment. Furthermore, Iran remains constrained by these more limited kinds of relationships. As the example of the NDF illustrates, Iran can go only so far with money, arms, and smarts if operating in a context shaped by locals, where it does not have the same geographic proximity or full ideological convergence.

Even though such limitations tend to check Iranian ambitions, Iran's interactions with nonstate groups have proven strategically significant and a major amplifier of Iranian influence. In the landscape of contemporary conflict and intervention, Iranian-backed hybrid actors have proven much more reliable and predictable from the perspective of their patron and not prone to outflanking Iran or surprising it. While Iran has experienced setbacks in the form of failed efforts at support and engagement and ruptures of relations, its failures have not proven destabilizing to the regime or the state.

It should also be noted that the scope of ambitions will influence the possibilities for success in cultivating nonstate groups. The challenges in institution-building on a national scale differ in material ways from substate efforts focused on nonstate and hybrid groups. Hybridity explains the success of some of Iran's ventures in the region—it is possible to cultivate an enduring hybrid by weakening a state by supporting competing alternatives. It is far harder to build a strong state in a context where the state is already significantly eroded. In practice, for example, it has been easier to build the PMU's ragtag band of hybrid militias than to build an effective national police force under the Ministry of the Interior—both ventures that Iran has attempted to support in Iraq, with unequal results. Similarly, it is easier to support Hezbollah than to help build an effective national army in Lebanon. Such examples might suggest the inherent weakness and limits of Iran's otherwise successful approach to cultivating hybrids.

The nature of Iranian efforts has also changed in recent years, taking on a much more significant transnational scope and focus. The transnational goals of Iranian-backed partners and proxies represent a new reality for Shia militancy and a new challenge for international policymakers. As the transnationalism of Shia militancy increases, it is worth considering whether this phenomenon will fundamentally alter the trajectory of radicalization among Shia militants and the tactics of Shia groups.

In contrast to these more successful models, the Sunni states of the region and other outside actors, like the United States, face serious challenges to their ability to establish or support effective nonstate or hybrid actors. Some regional states are investing heavily in support for nonstate groups; an example is the United Arab Emirates' activity in Yemen. But the institutional capacity of regional states continues to lag behind Iran's. Furthermore, the lack of an ideological framework for engaging with nonstate actors will continue to limit reliability and effectiveness of those efforts.

The track record of dealing with and engaging nonstate and hybrid actors should breed caution in those states who seek to advance policy aims in this fashion. Exigent circumstances and reluctance to intervene in military conflicts directly explain the rationale for doing so, but the outcomes of such engagements have at times undermined strategic goals or created more persistent longer-team challenges. Even in the best of circumstances, without serious oversight, strategic or ideological convergence, and a long-term commitment, the results of such efforts are unpredictable and potentially destabilizing.

The rise and outsized influence of hybrid actors reflects underlying state fragility. The power of hybrids now also poses a serious impediment to the reassertion of state authority and accountability. Many factors and outside sponsors have driven the proliferation of hybrids; they are not simply a function of Iranian regional policy. In today's complex conflict zones, hybrid actors form a distinct and significant reality. From a policy perspective, incremental approaches are more likely to yield results than proposals that seek to establish, or reestablish, clear unitary authority in conflict zones. However, past and current practice suggest that policy choices can influence the trajectory of hybrid actors, especially when policy takes into account the stateness and autonomy that distinguish hybrids from traditional proxies. The most viable path for managing hybrid actors lies in the state: patiently integrating hybrids into the state while reasserting state authority, competence, and accountability. Like other armed groups and nonstate actors, hybrids have thrived in a climate of regional dysfunction and conflict. At a regional and systemic level, only a renewed focus on conflict resolution, peacebuilding, and statebuilding can curtail the destructive impact of hybrid actors. Hybrids are but one manifestation of the vacuum left by eroded security and governance. Ultimately, the catastrophic impact of violent conflict remains the key driver of suffering and instability, and the central crisis for people of the region.

Notes

1. Stanford University's Armed Group Dataset, for instance, records information about the characteristics of approximately 1,570 armed groups active between 1970 and 2012 and is available at https://web.stanford.edu/~imalone/data.html.

2. For a discussion of the principle of stateness, see Francis Fukuyama, "The Missing Dimension of Stateness," in Francis Fukuyama, *State Building. Governance and World Order in the Twenty-First Century* (London: Profile Books, 2005) 1–57; and Nehal Bhuta, "Measuring Stateness, Ranking Political Orders: Indexes of State Fragility and State Failure," EUI Working Papers LAW No. 2012/32 (December 2012), https://ssrn.com/abstract=2201482 or http://dx.doi.org/10.2139/ssrn.2201482.

3. Renad Mansour and Peter Salisbury, "Between Order and Chaos: A New Approach to Stalled State Transformations in Iraq and Yemen," Chatham House, September 9, 2019, https://www.chathamhouse.org/publication/between-order-and-chaos-new-approach-stalled-state-transformations-iraq-and-yemen; Yezid Sayigh, "Hybridizing Security: Armies, Militias and Constrained Sovereignty," Carnegie Middle East Center, October 30, 2018, https://carnegie-mec.org/2018/10/30/hybridizing-security-armies-militias-and-constrained-sovereignty-pub-77597; Volker Boege, Anne Brown, Kevin Clements, and Anna Nolan, "On Hybrid Political Orders and Emerging States: State Formation in the Context of 'Fragility,'" Berghof Research Center for Constructive Conflict Management, 2008, https://www.berghof-foundation.org/fileadmin/redaktion/Publications/Handbook/Dialogue_Chapters/dialogue8_boegeetal_lead.pdf; and Renad Mansour, "The Popular Mobilisation Forces and the Balancing of Formal and Informal Power," *LSE Middle East Centre*, March 15, 2018, https://blogs.lse.ac.uk/mec/2018/03/15/the-popular-mobilisation-forces-and-the-balancing-of-formal-and-informal-power/.

4. "Office of the Coordinator for Reconstruction and Stabilization," U.S. Department of State Archive (2001–2009), https://2001-2009.state.gov/s/crs/.

5. Max Weber, "Politics as a Vocation," in *The Vocation Lectures*, ed. David Owen and Tracy B. Strong (Indianapolis: Hackett Publishing Company, 2004), 33.

6. Michael Mann, "The Autonomous Power of the State: Its Origins, Mechanisms and Results," *European Journal of Sociology/Archives européennes de sociologie* 25, no. 2 (1984): 185–213.

7. Charles Tilly, "Reflections on the History of European Statemaking" in *The Formation of National States in Western Europe*, ed. Charles Tilly (Princeton, NJ: Princeton University Press, 1975), 70.

8. Marina Ottaway, "Rebuilding State Institutions in Collapsed States," *Development and Change* 33, no. 5 (2002): 1001–23.

9. Robert H. Jackson, *Quasi-States: Sovereignty, International Relations and the Third World* (Cambridge: Cambridge University Press, 1991).

10. See for example Jackson, *Quasi-States*, 27–29.

11. Mann, "Autonomous Power of the State," 11.

12. This is not to say that the warlord does not engage in criminal or insurgent activity, as these categories overlap. But in general, the warlord's behavior is confined to this characterization.

13. A significant political science literature describes the different types of non-state actors, developing classifications that work across time periods and locations. As the scholars Ariel I. Ahram and Charles King argue, "the simultaneous claim to local supremacy but also a quasi-legal subservience and loyalty to superior authority" sets the warlord apart from other types of armed actors. Ahram and King, "The Warlord as Arbitrageur," *Theory and Society* 41, no. 2 (2012): 169–86. Kimberly Marten defines a warlord along four characteristics: "First, trained, armed men take advantage of the disintegration of central authority to seize control small slices of territory. Second, their actions are based on self-interest, not ideology. Third, their authority is based on charisma and patronage followers. Fourth, this personalistic rule leads to the fragmentation and economic arrangements across the country, disrupting the trade and making commerce and investment unpredictable." She argues, "Warlordism works and endures as a system because it brings profit to powerful people who keep the population sufficiently satisfied to prevent rebellion." Marten, "Warlordism in Comparative Perspective," *International Security* 31, no. 3 (2006/2007): 41–73.

14. See, for example, Eric Hobsbawm, *Bandits* (New York: Dell Publishing, 1971).

15. Ahram and King, "The Warlord as Arbitrageur."

16. Erwin van Veen and Feike Fliervoet of Clingendael (the Netherlands Institute of International Relations), have thus defined hybrid actors as those that are "both autonomous of, and linked with, the government and (quasi-) governmental coercive organizations" and which "cooperate and compete with the government depending on overlap of interests between these organizations, their broader political platforms (if any) and the government." See van Veen and Fliervoet, "Dealing with Tools of Political (Dis)Order," Clingendael, December 2018, https://www.clingendael.org/sites/default/files/2018-12/dealing-with-tools-of-political-disorder.pdf.

17. Mansour and Salisbury, "Between Order and Chaos."

18. See the discussion in Renad Mansour and Christine van den Toorn, "The 2018 Iraqi Federal Elections: A Population in Transition?" London School of

Economics Middle East Centre, July 2018, http://eprints.lse.ac.uk/89698/7/MEC_ Iraqi-elections_Report_2018.pdf.

19. See Douglas A. Ollivant and Erica Gaston, "The Problem with the Narrative of 'Proxy War' in Iraq," *War on the Rocks*, May 31, 2019, https://warontherocks. com/2019/05/the-problem-with-the-narrative-of-proxy-war-in-iraq/.

20. This definition does not include those groups that are merely wings of the Quds Force of Iran's Islamic Revolutionary Guard Corps (IRGC), because those actors are not hybrid actors as such.

21. Tim Eaton, Christine Cheng, Renad Mansour, Peter Salisbury, Jihad Yazigi, and Lina Khatib, "Conflict Economies in the Middle East and North Africa," Chatham House, June 2019, https://www.chathamhouse.org/publication/conflict-economies-middle-east-and-north-africa.

22. Examples of non-hybrid actors that still have clear ideologies include the Islamic State and the YPG—though scholars might disagree, after careful study, about whether the YPG is actually hybrid.

23. See for example, Mohand Jabar, "The Moment of PMU Retaliation for the Killing of the Speicher Martyrs" [in Arabic], YouTube video, 4:04, March 15, 2015, https://www.youtube.com/watch?v=PhMeJhJGQuQ.

24. The PMU is also often referred to in English as the Popular Mobilization Forces (PMF).

25. Security analysts, interview with author, Baghdad, February 2019.

26. Article 9, Paragraph B, of the Constitution of Iraq states that "the formation of military militia outside the framework of the armed forces is prohibited." Moreover, all armed groups are meant to be part of either the Ministry of Defence or Ministry of Interior.

27. For more on the origins of the PMU, see Renad Mansour and Faleh A. Jabar, "The Popular Mobilization Forces and Iraq's Future," Carnegie Middle East Centre, April 28, 2017, https://carnegie-mec.org/2017/04/28/popular-mobilization-forces-and-iraq-s-future-pub-68810.

28. From the 1980s, the Badr Brigades, the military wing of the Supreme Council for Islamic Revolution in Iraq, served as an insurgent group that fought against Saddam Hussein's regime in Baghdad. Much of this fighting was done from neighboring Iran or via underground cells in southern Iraq.

29. Nicholas Krohley, *The Death of the Mehdi Army: The Rise, Fall, and Revival of Iraq's Most Powerful Militia* (Hurst: London, 2015).

30. Fanar Haddad, *Sectarianism in Iraq: Antagonistic Visions of Unity* (Hurst: London, 2011).

31. Faleh Jabar, Renad Mansour, and Abir Khaddaj, "Maliki and the Rest: A Crisis Within a Crisis," Iraq Institute for Strategic Studies, June 6, 2012.

32. Thanassis Cambanis, "Can Militant Cleric Moqtada al-Sadr Reform Iraq?" The Century Foundation, May 1, 2018, https://tcf.org/content/report/can-militant-cleric-moqtada-al-sadr-reform-iraq/.

33. These militias included Asa'ib Ahl al-Haq, Kata'eb Hezbollah al-Iraqiya, Kata'eb Sayyid al-Shuhada', Harakat Hezbollah al-Nujaba', Kata'eb al-Imam Ali, and Kata'eb Jund al-Imam.

34. Maliki also used these groups to help Iran protect the regime of Syrian president Bashar al-Assad.

35. Ali al-Dhafiri, Abdulhussein Sha'aban, and Yahya al-Kabisi, "Sectarianism and the Future of the Political System in Iraq" [in Arabic], *Al Jazeera*, April 25, 2013, https://www.aljazeera.net/programs/in-depth/2013/4/25/ الطائفية-ومستقبل-النظام-السياسي-في-العراق.

36. Abu Mahdi was formerly the head of Kata'eb Hezbollah al-Iraqiya from 2007 to 2014. As the de facto leader, and although his formal title is deputy chair of the Popular Mobilization Units Commission (Haya't al-Hashd al-Sha'abi)—the government body that manages the PMU and answers directly to the prime minister—he is responsible for all PMU military operations on the ground. However, the formal leadership is with the chairman of the NSC in the prime minister's office. The NSC represents the PMU to the West, but Abu Mehdi runs all operations.

37. These observations are based on author conversations with PMU leaders over several years.

38. Ali Al-Mawlawi, "Delays to Iraq's 2019 Budget Reflect Growing Political Deadlock," *LSE Middle East Centre*, January 14, 2019, https://blogs.lse.ac.uk/mec/2019/01/14/delays-to-iraqs-2019-budget-reflect-growing-political-deadlock/.

39. Interview with author, Kirkuk, March 2018.

40. Mansour and Salisbury, "Between Order and Chaos."

41. For example, he told the author a year prior to becoming prime minister, while at a conference at the University of Cambridge, that Maliki's dependence on militias was problematic.

42. "Letter Published from Abu Mehdi al-Muhandis to Prime Minister Haider al-Abadi" [in Arabic], *Baghdad Times*, October 21, 2015, https://www.baghdad-times.net/2015/10/21/بغداد-تايمز-تنشر-رسالة-ابو-مهدي-المهند/. See also AlAhad2TV, "Letter of al-Haj Abu Mahdi al-Muhandis to the Prime Minister," YouTube, October 22, 2015, https://www.youtube.com/watch?v=3ZeWDyWvm_A.

43. Executive Order 91 of 2016.

44. "The Law of the Popular Mobilization Units Commission Number 40 for the Year 2016" [in Arabic], Ministry of Justice, January 5, 2017.

45. Mansour and van den Toorn, "The 2018 Iraqi Federal Elections."

46. Mohammed al-Hashimi ("Abu Jihad"), interview with author, Baghdad, June 2019.

47. For instance, in Diyala in May 2015, the governorate council appointed a Badr official, Muthanna al-Tamimi, as governor. In his position, the governor supports and praises the role of Ameri and the PMU in maintaining the security in Diyala. In Mosul, the PMU worked to appoint the new governor Mansour Marid,

who was part of Falih Alfayyadh's bloc—a part of the PMU's Binaa government bloc. The local police have complained to the author that they have not been able to hold either the governor or his PMU allies in Diyala to account. See "Governor of Basra, All Are Determined to Keep the Security File in the Hands of the Army, Police, and PMU, PMC" [in Arabic], PMU website, January 30, 2019, http://al-hashed. net/2019/01/30/محافظ-ديالى-الكل-مصمم-على-بقاء-الملف-ال/.

48. Several sources in Baghdad corroborated this point for one of the authors.

49. "The Basra Crisis: Sadr and Amiri Flip the Table on Abadi" [in Arabic], DW.com, September 8, 2018, https://www.dw.com/ar/أزمة-البصرة-الصدر-والعامري-يقلبان-الطاولة-على-العبادي/a-45412399.

50. Mansour and van den Toorn, "The 2018 Iraqi Federal Elections."

51. "Lack of Responsiveness Impacts Mood August—September 2015 Survey Findings," National Democratic Institute, November 23, 2015, https://www.ndi.org/sites/default/files/August%202015%20Survey_NDI%20Website.pdf.

52. See the group's website at http://al-hashed.net/.

53. Author interviews in Basra, February 2019.

54. PMU Commission official, interview with author, Baghdad, February 2019.

55. Senior Badr Organization official, interview with author, Baghdad, April 2018.

56. The Sunni contingents include Brigades 51, 56, 88, 90, 91, and 92; the Sha-bak, Brigade 30; the Turkmen, Brigade 16; the Yazidi, Brigade 36; and the Christian, Brigade 50.

57. Parts of the governorate of Diyala, for instance, remain vulnerable to attacks from groups like the Islamic State. In 2019, in the town of Buhriz, near Baqubah, the Islamic State has increased its attacks on local security forces, tribal leaders, and private sector sites. In July 2019, the PMU ran a campaign called the "Will of Victory" (Iradat al-Nasr), which included thirteen PMU brigades fighting the Islamic State in parts of Diyala, Salahaddin, Nineveh, and northern Baghdad.

58. Author's interview by phone with PMF official, August 2019.

59. "Baghdad: Biggest Mafia Chief Arrested," BasNews, August 6, 2019, http://www.basnews.com/index.php/en/news/iraq/538220.

60. "The PMU Takes Control of 4 Oil Smuggling Tanks in Southern Mosul" [in Arabic], PMU website, August 6, 2019, http://al-hashed.net/2019/08/06/الحشد-يسيطر-على-أربعة-صهاريج-صهاريج-لتهريب-ال/.

61. Renad Mansour, "Why Are Iraq's Paramilitaries Turning on Their Own Ranks?" Washington Post, February 18, 2019, https://www.washingtonpost.com/news/monkey-cage/wp/2019/02/18/why-are-iraqs-paramilitaries-turning-on-their-own-ranks/.

62. Renad Mansour, "Iraq's Paramilitaries Are Turning on Their Own Ranks," Chatham House, February 26, 2019, https://www.chathamhouse.org/expert/comment/iraq-s-paramilitaries-are-turning-their-own-ranks.

63. According to sources in the prime minister's office at the time.

64. Civil servant in Diyala provincial council, interview with author, February 2019.

65. Mustafa Saadoun, "Basra Residents Reeling from Contaminated Drinking Water," *Al-Monitor*, August 31, 2018, https://www.al-monitor.com/pulse/originals/2018/08/iraq-basra-health-water.html.

66. "The PMU's Engineering Efforts Begin by Extending Pipes to Deliver Water to More Than Eleven Areas in Basra" [in Arabic], PMU website, November 13, 2018, http://al-hashed.net/2018/11/13/أن-يمد-تباشر-للحشد-الهندسي-الجهد-آليات/.

67. For instance, in July 2019 the PMU website published that Barak al-Shammarri, who heads Najaf's electricity distribution department, asked Tahir al-Khaqani, who heads Firqat al-Imam Ali al-Qitaliya (PMU Brigade 2) for help from the PMU in "serving the people of the holy province" by helping to coordinate electricity supply and offer his brigade's manpower in this effort. See "Najaf Electric Requests the Help of the PMU to Better Serve the People of the Governorate" [in Arabic], PMU website, July 1, 2019, http://al-hashed.net/2019/07/01/لتقديم-الحشد-مساعدة-تطلب-النجف-كهرباء/.

68. In February 2019, the PMU website published a story about one of its brigades rescuing a family that was injured in a traffic accident in the Saadiya subdistrict of the governorate of Diyala. "The PMU Save a Family Injured in a Traffic Accident in Diyala" [in Arabic], PMU website, February 22, 2019, http://al-hashed.net/2019/02/22/سي-بحادث-أصيبت-عائلة-ينقذ-الشعبي-الحشد/.

69. "The PMU Saves 40 Thousand Acres between Maysan and Basra from Drowning" [in Arabic], The Iraqi News Agency, February 15, 2019, http://www.ina.iq/81597/والبصرة-ميسان-بين-الغرق-من-دونم-الف-40--ينقذ-الحشد. See also "The Engineering Unit of the PMU Fixes the Streets of the Kerma Ali Area in Basra" [in Arabic], *Shafaqna News*, January 5, 2019, https://iq.shafaqna.com/EN/AL/3056695.

70. " PMU Military Engineering Dries the Areas of the Diyala Bridge" [in Arabic], PMU website, February 9, 2019, http://al-hashed.net/2019/02/09/من-تغيث-الشعبي-للحشد-العسكرية-الهندسة/.

71. "[Abu Mahdi] al-Muhandis Visits a New Plant in Basra" [in Arabic], PMU website, January 20, 2019, http://al-hashed.net/2019/01/20/معمل-يزور-المهندس بالبص-والصلب-الحديد/; and Sophia Barbarani, "Once Prized Across the Middle East, Iraq's Dates Industry Clings to Hope of Better Days," *National*, June 28, 2018, https://www.thenational.ae/world/mena/once-prized-across-the-middle-east-iraq-s-dates-industry-clings-to-hope-of-better-days-1.744966.

72. Civil servant in Diyala governorate council, interview with author, February 2019; author interviews with residents in Diyala, February 2019; and "The PMU in Basra Rebuilds a Number of Schools in the Province" [in Arabic], PMU website, November 29, 2018, http://al-hashed.net/2018/11/29/في-المدارس-من-عددا-يرمم-البصرة-في-الحشد/.

73. Interview with author, Baghdad, June 2019.

74. Civil society activists, interview with author, Basra, February 2019.

75. Interview with author, Baghdad, spring 2018.

76. Munqith al-Dagher, "Iran's Influence in Iraq Is Declining. Here's Why," *Washington Post*, November 16, 2018, https://www.washingtonpost.com/news/monkey-cage/wp/2018/11/16/irans-influence-in-iraq-is-declining-heres-why/.

77. For more on these trends, see Fanar Haddad, "The Waning Relevance of the Sunni–Sunni Divide," The Century Foundation, April 10, 2019, https://tcf.org/content/report/waning-relevance-sunni-shia-divide/.

78. Tamer El-Ghobashy and Mustafa Salim, "Chanting 'Iran, Out!' Iraqi Protesters Torch Iranian Consulate in Basra," *Washington Post*, September 7, 2018, https://www.washingtonpost.com/world/chanting-iran-out-iraqi-protesters-torch-iranian-consulate-in-basra/2018/09/07/2caa89b8-b2bd-11e8-8b53-50116768e499_story.html.

79. Some authors and diplomats characterize such shifts away from being a proxy as a "convergence of interest" model. This model gives greater agency to the Iraqi hybrid armed actor who has to balance orders from Iran—as a proxy—with meeting the demands of his constituents and succeeding in local politics. As Ollivant and Gaston argue, "Iraqi actors tended to explain [in the authors' research] their behavior in terms of local competition, not the desires of foreign patrons." See Ollivant and Gaston, "The Problem with the Narrative of 'Proxy War' in Iraq."

80. Ranj Alaaldin, "Iran Used the Hezbollah Model to Dominate Iraq and Syria," *New York Times*, March 30, 2018, https://www.nytimes.com/2018/03/30/opinion/iran-hezbollah-iraq-syria.html.

81. Jeffrey Feltman, "Hezbollah: Revolutionary Iran's Most Successful Export," Brookings, January 17, 2019, brookings.edu/opinions/hezbollah-revolutionary-irans-most-successful-export/.

82. H. E. Chehabi, ed., *Distant Relations: Iran and Lebanon in the Last 500 Years* (London: I. B. Tauris, 2006).

83. On Sadr and on other aspects of Hezbollah's history discussed in this section, see, for example, Fouad Ajami, *The Vanished Imam: Musa al Sadr and the Shia of Lebanon* (Ithaca, NY: Cornell University Press, 1987); Nicholas Blanford, *Warriors of God: Inside Hezbollah's Thirty-Year Struggle against Israel* (New York: Random House, 2011); and Thanassis Cambanis, *A Privilege to Die: Inside Hezbollah's Legions and Their Endless War against Israel* (New York: Simon and Schuster, 2010).

84. Giorgio Cafiero and Peter Certo, "Hamas and Hezbollah Agree to Disagree on Syria," *MENASource*, Atlantic Council, January 30, 2014, https://www.atlanticcouncil.org/blogs/menasource/hamas-and-hezbollah-agree-to-disagree-on-syria.

85. Muhannad Hage Ali, "Power Points Defining the Syria-Hezbollah Relationship," Carnegie Middle East Center, March 29, 2019, https://carnegie-mec.org/2019/03/29/power-points-defining-syria-hezbollah-relationship-pub-78730.

86. Thanassis Cambanis, "The Israel-Hezbollah Channel: UNIFIL's Effective but Limited Conflict-Management Mechanism," in *Order from Ashes: New Foundation for Security in the Middle East*, ed. Michael Wahid Hanna and Thanassis Cambanis (New York: The Century Foundation, 2018), 56–78.

87. "Takfiri," a pejorative label for Sunni extremists, has been widely adopted by opponents, such as Hezbollah. "Takfiri" literally refers to a Muslim who proclaims another Muslim to be an apostate or "kafir" (infidel).

88. Rola el-Husseini, "Resistance, Jihad, and Martyrdom in Contemporary Lebanese Shi'a Discourse," *Middle East Journal* 62, no. 3 (2008): 399–414.

89. "Sayyed Nasrallah's Full Speech on the Islamic Resistance Support Organization Honorary Ceremony (Part 1)," *Alahed News*, May 6, 2016, https://english.alahednews.com.lb/essaydetails.php?eid=33345&cid=570#.WfLYRBOCyV4.

90. "Full Speech Delivered by Hizbullah Secretary General, His Eminence Sayyed Nasrallah, on the Divine Victory Anniversary Ceremony Held in Bint Jbeil on August 13, 2016," *Alahed News*, https://english.alahednews.com.lb/essaydetails.php?eid=34603&cid=570#.WfLYNxOCyV4. Hezbollah often capitalizes "Resistance" in its English communications.

91. Amal Saad-Ghorayeb, *Hizbu'llah: Politics and Religion* (London: Pluto, 2002); and Phillip Smyth, "Hizbullah Cavalcade," *Jihadology*, accessed September 10, 2019, http://jihadology.net/hizballah-cavalcade/.

92. ShiaTV, "[1/4] Hazrat Abbas Martyrdom Karbala | Al-Manar | Stories for Children—Arabic," ShiaTV.net, October 5, 2016, https://www.shiatv.net/video/452939213; and "Prophet Saleh (as) - FULL | Al-Manar | Eng Subs | Stories for Children," published to the YouTube channel For the Mahdi, April 6, 2015, https://www.youtube.com/watch?v=NuFri8No8WI.

93. See, for example, Al-Manar TV, http://english.almanar.com.lb/, particularly "Secretary General Hassan Nasrallah speeches on Al Manar TV," https://english.almanar.com.lb/cat/news/lebanon/s-nasrallah-speeches; Al-Nour Radio, http://www.alnour.com.lb/; and *Alahed News*, https://www.alahednews.com.lb/. Private channels include Electronic Resistance (@ResistanceER) on Twitter, https://twitter.com/resistanceer?lang=en; *Janoubia* http://janoubia.com/; and *Al Mayadeen* (and its television station), http://www.almayadeen.net/. All sites accessed September 10, 2019.

94. Blanford, *Warriors of God*.

95. Joseph Daher, *Hezbollah: The Political Economy of Lebanon's Party of God* (London: Pluto, 2016).

96. "Treasury Targets Iranian-Backed Hizballah Officials for Exploiting Lebanon's Political and Financial System," press release, U.S. Department of the Treasury, July 9, 2019, https://home.treasury.gov/news/press-releases/sm724.

97. Général Michel Aoun and Hassan Nasrallah, "Memorandum of Understanding by Hezbollah and Free Patriotic Movement," Voltaire Network, Beirut, February 6, 2006, https://www.voltairenet.org/article163916.html.

98. Na'īm Qāsim, *Hizbullah: The Story From Within* (London: Saqi Books, 2010).

99. The mechanics of patronage distribution have changed little since the end of the Lebanese Civil War, although the composition of the alliances has shifted over time. See Ramez Dagher, "Let the Wookie Win," *Moulahazat*, February 3, 2019, https://moulahazat.com/2019/02/03/let-the-wookie-win/.

100. Rodger Shanahan, *The Shi'a of Lebanon: Clans, Parties and Clerics* (London: I. B. Tauris, 2005); and Augustus Richard Norton, *Amal and the Shi'a: Struggle for the Soul of Lebanon* (Austin: University of Texas Press, 1987).

101. See Augustus Richard Norton, *Hezbollah: A Short History* (Princeton, NJ: Princeton University Press, 2007); Norton, *Amal and the Shi'a*; Judith Palmer Harik, *Hezbollah: The Changing Face of Terrorism* (London: I. B. Tauris, 2005); and, for the narrative from Hezbollah's own perspective, Qāsim, *Hizbullah*.

102. "Sayyed Nasrallah's Full Speech on International Al-Quds Day, 2019," *Alahed News*, May 31, 2019, https://english.alahednews.com.lb/48404/582.

103. "Hezbollah Secretary-General Nasrallah: Victories in Many Battlefields Owed to Iran," *Kayhan*, February 12, 2019, http://kayhan.ir/en/news/63069/victories-in-many-battlefields-owed-to-iran.

104. "Lebanon to Boycott Warsaw Conference Seen as Hostile to Iran," Associated Press, February 11, 2019, https://www.apnews.com/6e03112ffbf943648d19990 b18d931e0.

105. "Hezbollah Calls on Supporters to Donate as Sanctions Pressure Bites," Reuters, March 8, 2019, https://www.reuters.com/article/us-lebanon-hezbollah/hezbollah-calls-on-supporters-to-donate-as-sanctions-pressure-bites-idUSKCN1QP258.

106. See Ali Hashem, "Iran's Post-ISIS Regional Strategy," *Turkish Policy Quarterly*, Fall 2017, http://turkishpolicy.com/article/884/irans-post-isis-regional-strategy; and Ali Hashem, "Hezbollah's Journey from Syria's Battlefield to Lebanon's Political Minefield," Carnegie Middle East Center, August 28, 2018, https://carnegie-mec.org/2018/08/28/hezbollah-s-journey-from-syria-s-battlefield-to-lebanon-s-political-minefield-pub-77115.

107. Mona Alami, "Hezbollah's Evolving Role in Syria and Lebanon," *MENASource*, Atlantic Council, November 29, 2018, https://www.atlanticcouncil.org/blogs/menasource/hezbollah-s-evolving-role-in-syria-and-lebanon

108. Omar al-Sheikh, "The State's Gunmen: The Auxiliary Army" [in Arabic], *Al-Akhbar*, October 23, 2013, https://www.al-akhbar.com/Syria/59325.

109. Aron Lund, "Chasing Ghosts: The Shabiha Phenomenon," in *The Alawis of Syria: War, Faith and Politics in the Levant*, ed. Michael Kerr and Craig Larkin (London: Hurst & Co., 2015).

110. Syrian military intelligence defector, interview with author, Paris, June 2018.

111. Aziz Nakkash [Kheder Khaddour], "The Alawite Dilemma in Homs: Survival, Solidarity and the Making of a Community," Friedrich Ebert Foundation, March 2013, https://library.fes.de/pdf-files/iez/09825.pdf, 12.

112. Hicham Bou Nassif, "'Second-Class': The Grievances of Sunni Officers in the Syrian Armed Forces," *Journal of Strategic Studies* 38, no. 5 (2015): 626–49.

113. United Nations Human Rights Council (UNHCR), "Oral Update of the Independent International Commission of Inquiry on the Syrian Arab Republic," A/HRC/22/CRP.1, March 11, 2013, https://www.ohchr.org/Documents/HRBodies/HRCouncil/CoISyria/PeriodicUpdate11March2013_en.pdf, 3.

114. One member of the clan, Hassan Berri, was a member of the Syrian parliament, while another, Ali Zeineddine Berri, reportedly controlled part of Aleppo's criminal underworld. In July 2012, when Qatar- and Turkey-backed Sunni Islamists seized the eastern half of Aleppo, the Bab al-Nairab militias were overpowered and destroyed. Ali Zeineddine Berri was executed and his brother, Hassan, reportedly was wounded as he fled the fighting. "Zeinou Berri Martyred in Aleppo and Member of People's Council Hassan Shaaban Berri Wounded" [in Arabic], *Cham Times*, August 1, 2012, accessed June 17, 2014 (page discontinued).

115. Sam Dagher, "Syrian Conflict Draws in Christians," *Wall Street Journal*, July 23, 2012, online.wsj.com/article/SB10001424052702303644004577524653025270434.html.

116. Aron Lund, "Assad's Broken Base: The Case of Idlib," The Century Foundation, July 14, 2016, https://tcf.org/content/report/assads-broken-base-case-idlib.

117. Stathis N. Kalyvas, *The Logic of Violence in Civil War* (Cambridge, UK: Cambridge University Press, 12th print., 2013), 108.

118. UNHRC, "Oral Update," 3.

119. UNHRC, "Report of the Independent International Commission of Inquiry on the Syrian Arab Republic," A/HRC/21/50, August 16, 2012, https://www.ohchr.org/Documents/HRBodies/HRCouncil/RegularSession/Session21/A-HRC-21-50_en.pdf.

120. "Homs Governorate Police Leadership Ends the Work of the Neighborhood Committees and the Popular Committees" [in Arabic], *al-Ourouba*, April 20, 2011 (page discontinued).

121. "From the Ground: Civilians in the Army's Trench" [in Arabic], *Al Mayadeen*, March 21, 2013, www.almayadeen.net/episodes/640685/مدنيون-في-خندق-الجيش_ .

122. Erika Solomon, "Insight: Syrian Government Guerrilla Fighters Being Sent to Iran for Training," Reuters, April 4, 2013, https://www.reuters.com/article/us-syria-iran-training-insight/insight-syrian-government-guerrilla-fighters-being-sent-to-iran-for-training-idUSBRE9330DW20130404; Anonymous and Erika Solomon, "Battered by War, Syrian Army Creates Its Own Replacement," Reuters, April 21, 2013, https://www.reuters.com/article/us-syria-crisis-paramilitary-insight/insight-battered-by-war-syrian-army-creates-its-own-replacement-idUSBRE93K02R20130421.

123. National Defence Forces Facebook page, accessed September 13, 2019, https://www.facebook.com/National.Defence.Forces.NDF.

124. Anonymous and Erika Solomon, "Fearful Alawites Pay Sectarian Militias in Battered Homs," Reuters, September 25, 2012, https://www.reuters.com/article/us-syria-shabbiha-extortion/fearful-alawites-pay-sectarian-militias-in-battered-homs-idUSBRE88O0QD20120925; and Nakkash [Kheder Khaddour], "The Alawite Dilemma in Homs," 9–10.

125. Aryn Baker, "Syria's Assad May Be Losing Control Over His Deadly Militias," *Time*, September 11, 2013, world.time.com/2013/09/11/syrias-assad-may-be-losing-control-over-his-deadly-militias.

126. On the involvement of Sunni clerics and businessmen in parliamentary elections, see, for example, Thomas Pierret, *Religion and State in Syria: The Sunni Ulama from Coup to Revolution* (Cambridge, UK: Cambridge University Press, 2013), 152ff. On the most recent local elections, see Agnès Favier and Marie Kostrz, "Local Elections: Is Syria Moving to Reassert Central Control?" European University Institute, February 2019, https://cadmus.eui.eu/handle/1814/61004.

127. Favier and Kostrz, "Local Elections," 14. Given that most of Raqqa was at that time under the control of the US-backed, Kurdish-led Syrian Democratic Forces, the council is unlikely to wield much power at the moment.

128. "Final Results of the 2016 Parliamentary Elections" [in Arabic], SANA, April 16, 2016, https://www.sana.sy/?p=370333; and "Members of the Party's Central Committee," Ba'ath Party website, November 27, 2018, www.baathparty. sy/Posts.php?id=668. Wardeh's role as an NDF leader is clear from the Facebook page of the Salamiyah NDF (https://www.facebook.com/national.defence.salmiyah, accessed June 29, 2019), and also has been reported in the Syrian state press. See, for example, "350 Participate" [in Arabic], *al-Thawra*, March 26, 2017, archived at https://web.archive.org/web/20170326192748/http://thawra.sy/_print_veiw.asp? FileName=89013927820170326001340.

129. Nour Samaha, "The Black Market Kings of Damascus," *Atlantic*, October 3, 2016, https://www.theatlantic.com/international/archive/2016/10/syria-war-economy-damascus-assad/502304.

130. The other 51 percent of the company reportedly was owned by one Lawrence Halaw. See the al-Iqtisadi business database on https://aliqtisadi.com.

131. "Warlords Increasingly Integrating into Syria's Formal Economy," *Syria Report*, May 15, 2018, https://www.syria-report.com/news/economy/warlords-increasingly-integrating-syria's-formal-economy. The financial news site *al-Iqtisadi* (aliqtisadi. com) lists the company's owners as Bassam Ali Hassan (40%), Saqr Asaad al-Rustom (40%), Rim Munir Jaber (10%), and Khodr Asaad al-Rustom (10%). A note of caution: although *The Syria Report* identifies Saqr al-Rustom's main co-owner as being his NDF-linked uncle, Hassan, several other sources have named the latter as Bassam Merhaj al-Hassan, not Bassam Ali Hassan.

132. "Social Affairs and Martyr Foundation: Development Programs for the Families of Martyrs and War Wounded" [in Arabic], *Tishreen*, April 27, 2014, archive. tishreenonline.sy/index.php/محليات-/9048الشؤون-الاجتماعية-ومؤسسة-الشهيد-برامج-تنمية-لعائلات-الشهداء-وجرحى-الحرب. Rustom remains involved with the Martyr Foundation in 2019, as noted in "Opening of a Public Library for Children in Tartous" [in Arabic], *al-Wehda*, March 20, 2019, wehda.alwehda.gov.sy/first-page/137089-2019-03-19-15-33-28.html. The Martyr Foundation is called "Muassasat al-Shahid" in Arabic. There are strong indications that Nael al-Rustom is Saqr al-Rustom's brother. Both men appear to be of roughly similar age and are from, or have been based in, the same Homs neighborhood, al-Zahraa. Fuller versions of their names (Nael Asaad al-Rustom and Saqr Asaad al-Rustom) indicate that both are sons of a man named Asaad.

133. "Social Affairs and Martyr Foundation," *Tishreen*.

134. Martyr Foundation website, May 26, 2017, archived by the Internet Archive's Wayback Machine, accessed July 10, 2019, https://web.archive.org/web/20170526131148/http://shaheed-sy.org/Customer/Details/1.

135. "Syrian Martyr Foundation and the Social Survey Operation" [in Arabic], *al-Thawra*, June 23, 2013, http://archive.thawra.sy/_archive.asp?FileName=751448130201306022184739; and Amal Farhat, "Martyr Foundation," *Syria Times*, February 24, 2014, syriatimes.sy/index.php/society/11639-martyr-foundation.

136. "Sama Channel Meets with the Director of the Syrian Martyr Foundation," Sama TV broadcast from October 2013, published to the Martyr Foundation YouTube channel, June 20, 2015, https://www.youtube.com/watch?v=1-SMnps0IAY.

137. Kheder Khaddour, "Securing the Syrian Regime," *Sada*, Carnegie Endowment for International Peace, June 3, 2014, https://carnegieendowment.org/sada/55783.

138. Abdullah Suleiman Ali, "Fifth Corps: Coordination by Quartet . . . and an "Ornamented Ring" from Hezbollah" [in Arabic], *As-Safir*, November 28, 2016.

139. Khaddour, "Securing the Syrian Regime."

140. Wa'el Hefyan, "Syria's Martyrs . . . Records Full of Sacrifice . . . Blood Fencing in the Borders of the Homeland . . . and Institutions Caring for Their Rights" [in Arabic], *Jouhina* 90 (October 15, 2016), https://jouhina.com/magazine/files/PDF/90.pdf.

141. Ibid.

142. "Rigging the System: Government Policies Co-Opt Aid and Reconstruction Funding in Syria," Human Rights Watch, June 28, 2019, https://www.hrw.org/report/2019/06/28/rigging-system/government-policies-co-opt-aid-and-reconstruction-funding-syria.

143. Reinoud Leenders and Antonio Giustozzi, "Outsourcing State Violence: The National Defence Force, 'Stateness' and Regime Resilience in the Syrian War," *Mediterranean Politics* 23, no. 1 (2018): 2.

144. Kheder Khaddour, interview with author by phone, September 2018.

145. We have not been able to identify any NDF leader at the more senior ranks of major-general ("liwa") or lieutenant-general ("imad").

146. Kheder Khaddour, "The Coast in Conflict: Migration, Sectarianism, and Decentralization in Syria's Latakia and Tartus Governorates," Friedrich Ebert Stiftung, July 2016, https://library.fes.de/pdf-files/iez/12682-20160725.pdf, 14.

147. Mohammad D., interview with author by Skype, June 2013; Mohammad D., "Who Was Hilal al-Assad?" *Syria Comment*, April 5, 2014, http://www.joshualandis.com/blog/hilal-al-assad-mohammad-d.

148. Khaddour, interview, September 2018; Nour Nader, "Changes in the National Defence Leadership in Suwayda before the Battle of the South" [in Arabic], *Enab Baladi*, June 24, 2018, https://www.enabbaladi.net/archives/236974.

149. Kheder Khaddour, "Consumed by War: The End of Aleppo and Northern Syria's Political Order," Friedrich Ebert Stiftung, October 2017, https://library.fes.de/pdf-files/iez/13783.pdf, 13; and Ayman Douri, "Aleppo NDF Leader Gives Dam Press an Exclusive Interview" [in Arabic], *Dam Press*, August 11, 2017, http://www.dampress.net/?page=show_det&category_id=6&id=80938.

150. Nour Samaha, "How These Syrians Went from Opposition Fighters to Pro-Regime Militiamen," *Al-Monitor*, April 3, 2017, https://www.al-monitor.com/pulse/originals/2017/04/syria-south-opposition-defection-army-israel.html.

151. Circassians are a Sunni Muslim ethnic group historically from the Caucasus. In the nineteenth century, many Circassians fled Russian military campaigns to seek safety in the Ottoman Empire, of which Syria was then a part. Syrian Circassians traditionally live in the Golan Heights–Quneitra region, but many were displaced toward Damascus by Israel's occupation of the area in 1967.

152. "Death of Walid Abaza, One of the Regime's Most Prominent Security Officers, after a Chronic Illness" [in Arabic], *Al-Anba'*, October 15, 2017, https://www.alanba.com.kw/ar/arabic-international-news/syria-news/782527/15-10-2017 وفاة-وليد-أباظة-أحد-أبرز-ضباط-مخابرات-النظام-إثر-مرض-عضال-.

153. Rima Raei, "About the Most Beautiful Syrian Mothers: Of Sour Lemon, They Make Sweet Juice" [in Arabic], *Al-Akhbar*, August 11, 2015, https://al-akhbar.com/Syria/23835; and "The 'Mother of the Martyr' Group Is a Voluntary Labor Tracing Its Steps through the Societal and Human Fields" [in Arabic], SANA, December 22, 2015, https://sanasyria.org/?p=315676.

154. "Quneitra: UNDOF Returns and the Founder of the Golan Regiment Is Secretary of the Ba'ath Branch" [in Arabic], *Al-Modon*, August 10, 2017, https://www.almodon.com/print/607ac4ab-1f1e-41e5-95e1-487ce7b405af/16d51b21-d9ce-4a71-b543-e96dbb163bfb; and "Walid Abaza in God's Protection" [in Arabic], *Al-Hadath*, October 14, 2017, https://event.sy/SquareArticle-528.html. Khaled Abaza's dual role as NDF leader and Ba'ath chief has also been noted in the pro-government Damascus press and on the Ba'ath Party's official website; see "The Residents of Bureiqa, Bir Ajam, and Qahtaniya Reject Any Gunman Remaining in Their Towns" [in Arabic], *Al-Watan*, August 12, 2018, alwatan.sy/archives/162328; and "Comrade Dr Khaled Walid Abaza—Branch Secretary" [in Arabic], Ba'ath Party, February 7, 2019, baathparty.sy/Posts.php?id=906.

155. Leenders and Giustozzi, "Outsourcing State Violence."

156. Khaddour, interview.

157. Ibid.

158. Anonymous and Solomon, "Fearful Alawites Pay Sectarian Militias"; Anonymous and Solomon, "Syrian Army Creates Its Own Replacement"; and Nakkash [Khaddour], "The Alawite Dilemma in Homs," 9–10.

159. "The Most Important Legislative Measures and Special Decisions for the Families of the Martyrs and the Wounded" [in Arabic], Syrian Arab Republic Prime

Ministry, May 10, 2018, www.pministry.gov.sy/contents/13630/contents/13556/
أهم-التشريعات-والقرارات-الخاصة-بذوي-الشهداء--والجرحى.

160. "President Assad Issues a Law to Reserve 50 Percent of the Vacancies Intended to Be Filled through Trials and Tests for Families of Martyrs" [in Arabic], General Organization of Radio and Television, December 31, 2014, www.ortas.gov.sy/News/index.php?d=100349&id=166357.

161. "Government Prioritizes Allocation of Meagre Resources to Soldiers and Security Services Members," *Syria Report*, February 13, 2019, https://www.syria-report.com/news/economy/government-prioritizes-allocation-meagre-resources-soldiers-and-security-services-membe.

162. "The Toll of War: The Economic and Social Consequences of the Conflict in Syria," World Bank, 2017, https://www.worldbank.org/en/country/syria/publication/the-toll-of-war-the-economic-and-social-consequences-of-the-conflict-in-syria, 71.

163. UNHRC, "Report of the Independent International Commission of Inquiry on the Syrian Arab Republic," A/HRC/25/65, February 12, 2014, https://www.ohchr.org/EN/HRBodies/HRC/RegularSessions/Session25/Documents/A-HRC-25-65_en.doc, 33.

164. Rim Turkmani, Mary Kaldor, Wisam Elhamwi, Joan Ayo, and Nael Hariri, "Hungry for Peace: Positives and Pitfalls of Local Truces and Ceasefires in Syria," London School of Economics, 2014, http://www.lse.ac.uk/website-archive/newsAndMedia/PDF/Syriareport.pdf, 17.

165. Ibid., 18–19.

166. Sam Dagher, "Assad Intervenes to Try to Salvage Homs Humanitarian Mission," *Wall Street Journal*, February 12, 2014,https://www.wsj.com/articles/un-resumes-aid-mission-in-homs-1392215586.

167. Lauren Williams, "Fighting among Pro-Assad Groups Points to Factional Future," *Daily Star*, May 17, 2014, https://www.dailystar.com.lb/News/Middle-East/2014/May-17/256755-fighting-among-pro-assad-groups-points-to-factional-future.ashx.

168. Fares al-Shehabi, interview with author via online messaging service, June 2017.

169. Khaddour, "Consumed by War," 13; Aron Lund, "Aleppo Militias Become Major Test for Assad," *New Humanitarian*, June 22, 2017, www.thenewhumanitarian.org/analysis/2017/06/22/aleppo-militias-become-major-test-assad.

170. Interview with Khaldoun Abu Ali, published to Facebook by Radio al-Bayda' FM, September 10, 2017, https://www.facebook.com/albaydaa.fm/videos/1907853676142372.

171. Abu Ali, interview.

172. The U.S. sanctions designation originally referred to the new group as the "Popular Army" (al-Jaysh al-Sha'abi), but was later updated to include the

NDF branding. The Popular Army was the name of an older Ba'athist militia that appears to have been in severe disrepair by the start of the conflict. It is possible that remnants of that group were folded into the NDF alongside the popular committees, which may account for early confusion around its name. See "Treasury Sanctions Al-Nusrah Front Leadership in Syria and Militias Supporting the Asad Regime," U.S. Department of the Treasury, November 12, 2012, https://www.treasury.gov/press-center/press-releases/Pages/tg1797.aspx; and "Syria Designations Updates," U.S. Department of the Treasury, November 7, 2013, https://www.treasury.gov/resource-center/sanctions/OFAC-Enforcement/Pages/20130711.aspx.

173. Solomon, "Syrian Fighters Being Sent to Iran."

174. See Aron Lund, "The Making and Unmaking of Syria Strategy under Trump," The Century Foundation, November 29, 2018, https://tcf.org/content/report/making-unmaking-syria-strategy-trump.

175. An NDF leader from Homs who spoke to Al Mayadeen, a pro-Tehran television station in Beirut, denied that Iran had played any role in the creation of the NDF, and said that recruits were trained by "former officers who served in the armed forces and have experience." "From the Ground: Civilians in the Army's Trench" [in Arabic], Al Mayadeen, March 21, 2013, https://www.almayadeen.net/episodes/640685/مدنيون-في-خندق-الجيش_. Assad, too, described the NDF as a Syrian entity that in fact reduced his government's need for foreign fighters. "We have an army and we now have a National Defence that fights with the army, and its numbers are great," he told an interviewer from the state-owned daily *Al-Thawra* in July 2013. "No foreign party could provide such a number to fight alongside the armed forces." See "President Assad in Exclusive Interview with *Al-Thawra*" [in Arabic] *Al-Thawra*, July 4, 2013, https://archive.thawra.sy/_print_veiw.asp?FileName=63241515720130704021727.

176. Hamedani's recollections were published in a Persian-language book by Golali Babaei Peygham Mahi Ha, Tehran, 2015), who interviewed the IRGC commander before his death. The book has not been translated into English, but Arabic-language excerpts and commentary can be found in Fatima al-Samadi, "Message of the Month (Messages of the Fishes): What the Memoirs of General Hamedani Say: Iranian Protectorate over Syria," [in Arabic] *Siyasat Arabiya* 22 (September 2016), available via the Arab Center for Research and Policy Studies, https://siyasatarabiya.dohainstitute.org/ar/issue022/Documents/Siyassat22-2016_Issue.pdf, 137–42, and in several texts by Abdulrahman Alhaj, published in summer 2018 on Syria. tv. A few English-language quotes from the book are found in "Iran's Priorities in a Turbulent Middle East," Middle East & North Africa Report 184, International Crisis Group, April 2018, https://www.crisisgroup.org/middle-east-north-africa/gulf-and-arabian-peninsula/iran/184-irans-priorities-turbulent-middle-east.

177. Abdulrahman Alhaj suggests that this may be a reference to Mohsen Khodr, a Shia cleric from a village just east of Homs. Alhaj, "Recruitment of Alawites and

Shia to Repress the Revolution" [in Arabic], Syria TV, May 19, 2018, https://www. syria.tv/content/تجنيد-العلويين-والشيعة-لقمع-الثورة.

178. Excerpted in Abdulrahman Alhaj, "When Assad Thought of Fleeing Syria" [in Arabic], Syria TV, June 10, 2018, https://www.syria.tv/content/حين-فكر-بشار-الأسد-بالهروب-من-سوريا.

179. Ibid.

180. On January 18, 2013, Rousiya al-Yom, a Russian state television channel that broadcasts in Arabic, reported that a "National Defense Army" was about to be "formed by civilians who have completed their military service in addition to members of the popular committees that formed spontaneously as the current conflict developed in Syria." Days later, the channel released footage of female NDF recruits training in Homs, which triggered an avalanche of "female warriors"–themed reports in the Arab, Western, and international press. In March 2013, the Iran-friendly pro-Assad television channel Al Mayadeen ran an hour-long documentary that described the NDF as an indigenous Syrian project with roots in Homs. It was clear from the documentary that it had already long operated on the ground. "Source to Rousiya al-Yom: Syrian Authorities Intend to Create a National Defense Army to Protect Neighborhoods from the Gunmen" [in Arabic], Rousiya al-Yom, January 18, 2013, https://arabic.rt.com/news/605343; "Setting up the First Female Unit of the NDF" [in Arabic], Rousiya al-Yom, January 23, 2013, https://arabic.rt.com/news/605802; and "From the Ground: Civilians in the Army's Trench" [in Arabic], Al Mayadeen, March 21, 2013, www.almayadeen.net/episodes/640685/مدنيون-في-خندق-الجيش_.

181. Maalla died on December 11, 2015. Al-Rabita, no. 27, 2016, 43. A Facebook page that serves as an online memorial for Maalla has published a eulogy of a Hezbollah fighter named Hassan Ali Ismail (Hajj Siraj), described as a companion of Maalla, who appears to have been killed at the same time. Reports from Ismail's funeral in Lebanon make it evident that he was linked to Hezbollah. Post on Facebook by the account al-Shahid al-Muqaddam Ahmed Maalla Maalla, December 19, 2015 (page discontinued); Amer Ferhat, "In Pictures: Eastern Zouter and Hezbollah Mourned the Mujahed Martyr Hassan Ali Ismail, 'Seraj,' in Enormous Funeral" [in Arabic], Al-Nabatieh, December 13, 2015, nabatieh.org/news.php?go=fullnews&newsid=11258.

182. This report uses American English spellings for most translations of names, unless another translation has already been established. The National Defence Forces spells its name in the British style in translation, while the Local Defense Forces do not (and there are few if any examples of the LDF translating its name at all).

183. Aymenn al-Tamimi, "The Local Defence Forces: Regime Auxiliary Forces in Aleppo," Syria Comment, May 23, 2016, https://www.joshualandis.com/blog/local-defence-forces-regime-auxiliary-forces-aleppo; and Aymenn al-Tamimi, "Administrative Decisions on Local Defence Forces Personnel: Translation & Analysis," personal website of Aymenn Jawad Al-Tamimi, May 3, 2017, www.aymennjawad. org/2017/05/administrative-decisions-on-local-defence-forces.

184. "Tehran Urges Damascus to Legalize the NDF" [in Arabic], Rousiya al-Yom, November 23, 2017, https://ar.rt.com/jjcz.

185. Judah Ari Gross, "In Trilateral Jerusalem Summit, Russia Sides with Iran, against Israel and US," *Times of Israel*, June 25, 2019, https://www.timesofisrael.com/in-trilateral-summit-russia-sides-with-iran-against-israel-and-us.

186. Charles Ayoub, "Why the Shia Duo Does Not Break Apart and Its Alliance Continues to Increase" [in Arabic], *Addiyar*, January 11, 2018, http://www.lebanon files.com/news/1277294.

187. Shanahan, *The Shi'a of Lebanon*, 106.

188. Ibid.

189. Norton, *Amal and the Shi'a*, 62.

190. Ibid., 63.

191. Shanahan, *The Shi'a of Lebanon*, 113.

192. Norton, *Amal and the Shi'a*, 88–90.

193. Ibid., Appendix A; see also Shanahan, *The Shi'a of Lebanon*, 110.

194. Norton, *Amal and the Shi'a*, 82.

195. Shanahan, *The Shi'a of Lebanon*, 115.

196. Ibid., 119.

197. Gary C. Gambill and Daniel Nassif, "Lebanon's Parliamentary Elections: Manufacturing Dissent," *Middle East Forum* 2, no. 8 (2000), https://www.meforum.org/meib/articles/0009_l1.htm,

198. Mounir Al Rabih, "Bassil Is More Syrian than Berri, Who Is Now Suspect to Assad" [in Arabic], *Al Modon*, January 13, 2019, https://www.almodon.com/politics/2019/1/13/باسيل-أكثر-سورية-من-بري-المشبوه-عند-الأسد.

199. Saad Hariri quoted in Hussein Dakroub, "Dissociation Pact Ends Resignation," *Daily Star*, December 6, 2017, https://www.pressreader.com/lebanon/the-daily-star-lebanon/20171206/281479276746276.

200. "Mansour Openly Disobeys Lebanon President," *Ya Libnan*, July 25, 2012, https://yalibnan.com/2012/07/25/mansour-openly-disobeys-lebanon-president/; and Abbas Daher, "Has Berri Ever Left Syria?" [in Arabic], *Elnashra*, January 1, 2019, https://www.elnashra.com/news/show/1274217/وهل-ترك-بري-سوريا-يوما؟.

201. Norton, *Amal and the Shi'a*, 90.

202. Osama Habib, "Ministers on Controversial Visit to Damascus," *Daily Star*, August 17, 2017, https://www.pressreader.com/lebanon/the-daily-star-lebanon/20170817/281668255085950.

203. "Nabih Berri Is Surprised Syria Is Not Invited to the Arab Economic Summit" [in Arabic], website of Nabih Berri, December 10, 2018, http://www.nabih berry.com/الرئيس-بري-يستغرب-عدم-دعوة-سوريا-للقمة.

204. *ShiaWatch*, an online newspaper set up by a group of Lebanese Shia opposition activists and intellectuals (also known as "the Shia third way") criticizes the Shia duo's monopoly of Shia representation in Lebanon. In a commentary piece, the newspaper quoted a former senior Amal personality as using a military metaphor

for the two groups' relationship, saying that "Amal's constituency was 'occupied' to a large extent by Hezbollah." See "Alerts," *ShiaWatch*, February 9, 2015, http://www.shiawatch.com/article/610.

205. Lebanese Welfare Association for the Handicapped (LWAH), accessed September 13, 2019, https://www.lwah.org.lb/.

206. Daleel Madani, a well-known civil society website network in Lebanon, identifies the LWAH as a "non-governmental organization founded in 1984, and has special consultative status with the UN Economic and Social Council since the year 2000." See "Lebanese Welfare Association for the Handicapped," Daleel Madani, accessed September 13, 2019, https://www.daleel-madani.org/civil-society-directory/lebanese-welfare-association-handicapped/about. Also, LWAH has coordinated with the Water Resources and Development (WARD) contracting company to finish its Berri rehabilitation center. "Completion and Equipping of Nabih Berri Hospital Center Rehabilitation Compound in Sarafand," WARD, accessed September 13, 2019, http://www.wardlebanon.com/project.asp?pid=63.

207. "Chancellor," Phoenicia University, September 13, 2019, https://www.pu.edu.lb/chancellor.

208. Annahar Staff, "Berri's Amal Movement: Bassil's Remarks Threaten Lebanon's Unity," *An-Nahar*, January 29, 2018, https://en.annahar.com/article/743916-berris-amal-movement-bassils-remarks-threaten-lebanons-unity.

209. Michael Knights, "Last Man Standing: U.S. Security Cooperation and Kurdistan's Peshmerga," *Washington Institute Policy Watch* 2292, July 24, 2014, http://www.washingtoninstitute.org/policy-analysis/view/last-man-standing-u.s.-security-cooperation-and-kurdistans-peshmerga.

210. By the late 1980s, for instance, the KDP had 15,000 peshmerga fighters. Foreign Staff, "Kurds Urge Turkey to Let in Victims of Iraqi Gas," *The Financial Times*, August 30, 1988.

211. "Kurdistan Regional Government Ministers," Kurdistan Regional Government, April 6, 2012, http://previous.cabinet.gov.krd/a/d.aspx?s=010000&l=12&a=43524.

212. Iffat Idris, "Inclusive and Sustained Growth in Iraq," K4D Helpdesk Report, June 20, 2018, https://assets.publishing.service.gov.uk/media/5b6d747440f0b640b095e76f/Inclusive_and_sustained_growth_in_Iraq.pdf.

213. Ahmed Tabaqchalli, "The Debate Over Iraqi Kurdistan's Share of the Federal Budget," Al-Bayan Center for Planning and Studies, 2019, http://www.bayancenter.org/en/wp-content/uploads/2019/06/9876544.pdf.

214. "Iraqi Kurds Say Upgrade Raises Oil Pipeline Capacity to 1 Million BPD," Reuters, November 4, 2018, https://www.reuters.com/article/us-iraq-oil/iraqi-kurds-say-upgrade-raises-oil-pipeline-capacity-to-1-million-bpd-idUSKCN1N90MX.

215. Eaton et al., "Conflict Economies in the Middle East and North Africa."

216. For a detailed discussion of the parties' manipulation of nationalist sentiments to buoy their popularity, see Cale Salih and Maria Fantappie, "Kurdish Nationalism at an Impasse: Why Iraqi Kurdistan Is Losing Its Place at the Center of

Kurdayeti," The Century Foundation, April 29, 2019, https://tcf.org/content/report/iraqi-kurdistan-losing-place-center-kurdayeti/.

217. Barbara Slavin, "Iraqi Kurdish Officials Describe 'Different Country' after Mosul," *Al-Monitor*, July 2, 2014, https://www.al-monitor.com/pulse/originals/2014/07/us-kurdish-independence-hopes-baghdad-collapse-power-share.html.

218. "President Barzani: War with Islamic State may Escalate," *Hawler Times*, January 12, 2015, https://hawlertimes.com/2015/01/12/president-barzani-war-with-islamic-state-may-escalate/.

219. Article 110 (b) of the Constitution of Iraq (written in 2005).

220. Thomas E. Ricks, "Situation Called Dire in West Iraq Anbar is Lost Politically, Marine Analyst Says," *Washington Post*, September 11, 2006, https://www.washingtonpost.com/archive/politics/2006/09/11/situation-called-dire-in-west-iraq-span-classbankheadanbar-is-lost-politically-marine-analyst-saysspan/0d815991-c7fe-4aee-97ec-ba95ca9a5c00/.

221. Timothy S. McWilliams and Kurtis P. Wheeler, eds., *Al-Anbar Awakening, Volume I, American Perspectives: U.S. Marines and Counterinsurgency in Iraq, 2004–2009* (Quantico, VA: Marine Corps University Press, 2009) 1, https://www.hqmc.marines.mil/Portals/61/Docs/Al-AnbarAwakeningVolI[1].pdf.

222. Najim Abed Al-Jabouri and Sterling Jensen, "The Iraqi and AQI Roles in the Sunni Awakening," *PRISM* 2, no. 1, December 2010, https://cco.ndu.edu/Portals/96/Documents/prism/prism_2-1/Prism_3-18_Al-Jabouri_Jensen.pdf.

223. U.S. Department of Defense, "Measuring Stability and Security in Iraq," Report to Congress in accordance with the Department of Defense Supplemental Appropriations Act 2008, March 2009, https://dod.defense.gov/Portals/1/Documents/pubs/Measuring_Stability_and_Security_in_Iraq_March_2009.pdf.

224. Ibid.

225. Douglas A. Ollivant, "Countering the New Orthodoxy: Reinterpreting Counterinsurgency in Iraq," New America Foundation, June 2011, https://static.newamerica.org/attachments/4344-countering-the-new-orthodoxy/Ollivant_Reinterpreting_Counterinsurgency.5d769bb8f672493a9fd1086919de9f51.pdf.

226. Carter Malkasian, "Anbar's Illusions: The Failure of Iraq's Success Story," *Foreign Affairs*, June 24, 2017, https://www.foreignaffairs.com/articles/iraq/2017-06-24/anbars-illusions.

227. Ollivant, "Countering the New Orthodoxy," 2.

228. As Renad Mansour has written elsewhere, "Following the events of 2003 and the creation of the identity-based system, the Sunnis failed to unite in the same way as the Shia Islamist or Kurdish ethnonationalist groups. Lacking a political party or other forms of social authority (i.e. centralized religious leadership), the Sunnis had no long-serving institutional representation." See "Challenges to the Post-2003 Political Order in Iraq," Swedish Institute of International Affairs, August 2019, https://www.ui.se/globalassets/ui.se-eng/publications/ui-publications/2019/ui-paper-no.-8-2019.pdf.

229. Reidar Visser, "Iraq's New Government and the Question of Sunni Inclusion," *CTC Sentinel* 7, no. 9 (September 2014), https://ctc.usma.edu/iraqs-new-government-and-the-question-of-sunni-inclusion/.

230. Zaid al-Ali, "Iraq's Rot Starts at the Top," *New York Times*, August 10, 2014, https://www.nytimes.com/2014/08/11/opinion/iraq-s-rot-starts-at-the-top.html.

231. Visser, "Iraq's New Government and the Question of Sunni Inclusion."

232. Michael Knights, "The Status and Future of the Awakening Movements in Iraq," *Sada*, Carnegie Endowment for International Peace, June 2, 2009, https://carnegieendowment.org/sada/23190.

233. Al-Jabouri and Jensen, "The Iraqi and AQI Roles in the Sunni Awakening."

234. Michael Wahid Hanna, "The Reawakened Specter of Iraqi Civil War, *Middle East Report Online*, April 17, 2009, https://merip.org/2009/04/the-reawakened-specter-of-iraqi-civil-war/#[7].

235. "Some US-Backed Iraqi Militias Plotting Attacks—Vice President," *Daily Star*, April 15, 2009, http://www.dailystar.com.lb/ArticlePrint.aspx?id=82801&mode=print.

236. Tim Arango, "Iraqi Sunnis Frustrated as Awakening Loses Clout," *New York Times*, May 3, 2010, https://www.nytimes.com/2010/05/04/world/middleeast/04awakening.html.

237. James Kitfield, "Can Another 'Anbar Awakening' Save Iraq?" Defense One, February 3, 2014, https://www.defenseone.com/ideas/2014/02/can-another-anbar-awakening-save-iraq/78053/.

238. "Make or Break: Iraq's Sunnis and the State," International Crisis Group, Middle East Report no. 144, August 14, 2013, https://d2071andvip0wj.cloudfront.net/make-or-break-iraq-s-sunnis-and-the-state.pdf, 4.

239. Malkasian, "Anbar's Illusions."

240. Craig Whiteside, "Nine Bullets for the Traitors, One for the Enemy: The Slogans behind the Islamic State's Campaign to Defeat the Sunni Awakening (2006–2017)," International Centre for Counter-Terrorism—The Hague, September 7, 2018, https://icct.nl/wp-content/uploads/2018/09/ICCT-Whiteside-Nine-Bullets-For-The-Traitors-September-2018.pdf.

241. Suadad al-Salhy, "Al-Qaeda Strikes Fear into Iraq's Government-Backed Sunni Militia," Reuters, October 18, 2013, https://www.reuters.com/article/us-iraq-sahwa/al-qaeda-strikes-fear-into-iraqs-government-backed-sunni-militia-idUSBRE99H0DH20131018.

242. Loveday Morris, "To Retake Cities, Iraq Turns to Sunni Tribes," *Washington Post*, January 30, 2014, https://www.washingtonpost.com/world/middle_east/to-retake-cities-iraq-turns-to-sunni-tribes/2014/01/30/561a0a32-83b3-11e3-a273-6ffd9cf9f4ba_story.html.

243. "The Mujahideen Shura Council Announces the Founding of an Islamic Emirate in Iraq" [in Arabic], *Al Arabiya*, October 15, 2006, https://www.alarabiya.net/articles/2006/10/15/28296.html.

244. Abu Bakr al-Baghdadi, "Give Good News to the Believers" [in Arabic], Fur-qan Media, April 9, 2013 (accessed via Jihadology.net on August 15, 2019).

245. Aron Lund, "A Public Service Announcement from al-Qaeda," Carnegie Middle East Center, February 3, 2014, https://carnegie-mec.org/diwan/54411?lang=en.

246. Abu Mohammed al-Adnani, "This Is the Promise of Allah" [in Arabic], Furqan Media, June 29, 2014 (accessed via Jihadology.net on August 15, 2019), https://jihadology.net/2014/06/29/al-furqan-media-presents-a-new-audio-message-from-the-islamic-states-shaykh-abu-mu%E1%B8%A5ammad-al-adnani-al-shami-this-is-the-promise-of-god/. On Islamic State apocalypticism, see William McCants, *The ISIS Apocalypse: The History, Strategy, and Doomsday Vision of the Islamic State* (New York: St. Martin's Press, 2015).

247. Daniel Milton and Muhammad al-'Ubaydi, "Pledging Bay'a: A Benefit or Burden to the Islamic State?" *CTC Sentinel* 8, no. 3 (2015), https://ctc.usma.edu/pledging-baya-a-benefit-or-burden-to-the-islamic-state.

248. "Hosted by the Commander of the Believers" [in Arabic], Furqan Media, April 29, 2019 (accessed via Jihadology.net on August 15, 2019).

249. Ayman al-Zawahiri declared in 2008 that the Islamic State in Iraq represented "a step toward the establishment of the caliphate, which is superior to the mujahed groups; therefore, the groups [in Iraq] must pledge allegiance to the state and not the other way around." Asked to clarify al-Qaeda's relationship to the Islamic State, he said that it, the Islamic Emirate of Afghanistan (Taliban), and the Islamic Emirate of the Caucasus (Chechnya) were "Islamic emirates that do not follow any one leader," and that bin Laden and al-Qaeda served under the Islamic Emirate of Afghanistan. In the future, he said, a caliphate might arise that would subsume all these three emirates as well as nonstate Islamic groups and movements. See "The Open Meeting with Sheikh Ayman al-Zawahiri, Second Round" [in Arabic], *al-Sahab*, April 2008 (copy in author's possession). During the postsplit debate between al-Qaeda and the Islamic State in 2014, the Islamic State spokesperson and leader Abu Mohammed al-Adnani stated that since 2006 the group had "complied with al-Qaeda's order" to avoid attacking Iran, and, respecting al-Qaeda's wishes, had refrained from establishing itself in Saudi Arabia, Egypt, Libya, and elsewhere. See Abu Mohammed al-Adnani, "Apologies, Emir of al-Qaeda" [in Arabic], *Furqan Media*, May 11, 2014 (accessed via Jihadology.net on August 16, 2019).

250. Abu Bakr al-Qurashi, "Interview: Special Meeting with the Mujahideen of the Nineveh Governorate in the Islamic State" [in Arabic], *Sada al-Jihad*, February/March 2008, 15 (copy in author's possession). Ansar al-Islam was virtually wiped out through defections to the Islamic State in 2014. Aymenn Al-Tamimi, "The Islamic State (IS) and Pledges of Allegiance: The Case of Jamaat Ansar al-Islam," *Syria Comment*, November 28, 2014, https://www.joshualandis.com/blog/islamic-state-pledges-allegiance-case-jamaat-ansar-al-islam; and Aymenn Al-Tamimi, "A Complete History of Jamaat Ansar al-Islam," personal website of Aymenn

Al-Tamimi, December 15, 2015, https://www.aymennjawad.org/2015/12/a-complete-history-of-jamaat-ansar-al-islam..

251. Sudarsan Raghavan, "Sunni Factions Split with al-Qaeda Group," *Washington Post*, April 14, 2007, http://www.washingtonpost.com/wp-dyn/content/article/2007/04/13/AR2007041300294.html; and McCants, *The ISIS Apocalypse*, 33ff.

252. Baghdadi, "Give Good News to the Believers," 5. "Allah"—God—remains untranslated in the source material.

253. Cole Bunzel, "The Islamic State of Disunity: Jihadism Divided," *Jihadica*, January 30, 2014, www.jihadica.com/the-islamic-state-of-disunity-jihadism-divided.

254. Adnani, "This Is the Promise of Allah," 5, 7.

255. "The Legal ['shar'i'] Position on the Announcement of the Caliphate" [in Arabic], Syrian Muslim Brotherhood, July 5, 2014 (copy in author's possession).

256. Hassane Abboud, interview with author via online chat, July 2014.

257. Joas Wagemakers of Radboud University, interview with author via e-mail, July 2014.

258. The Islamic State "seeks to stimulate more than to convince," write Jessica Stern and J. M. Berger, contrasting the differing appeals of al-Qaeda's quest for "an idealized future that its leaders did not expect to see realized in their lifetime" with the Islamic State's rejection of this "fundamentally defeatist model" to instead "implement the future now." Stern and Berger, *ISIS: The State of Terror* (New York: HarperCollins, 2015), 194–95.

259. Rukmini Callimachi, "The ISIS Files: When Terrorists Run City Hall," *New York Times*, April 4, 2018, https://www.nytimes.com/interactive/2018/04/04/world/middleeast/isis-documents-mosul-iraq.html.

260. Ibid.; "Archive of Islamic State Administrative Documents," personal website of Aymenn Jawad Al-Tamimi, January 27, 2015, https://www.aymennjawad.org/2015/01/archive-of-islamic-state-administrative-documents.

261. In eastern Syria, the group reportedly "forced municipality personnel to work, unlike previous groups that had allowed Syrian state employees to continue to receive their salaries (mostly from the regime) while they sat at home and did nothing, no doubt with attendant kickbacks." Hassan Hassan and Michael Weiss, *ISIS: Inside the Army of Terror* (New York: Regan Arts, 2015), 232.

262. Callimachi, "The ISIS Files."

263. "Financing of the Terrorist Organization Islamic State in Iraq and the Levant (ISIL)," Financial Action Task Force, February 2015, www.fatf-gafi.org/topics/methodsandtrends/documents/financing-of-terrorist-organisation-isil.html.

264. Erika Solomon and Ahmed Mhidi, "Isis Inc: Syria's 'Mafia-Style' Gas Deals with Jihadis," *Financial Times*, October 15, 2015, https://www.ft.com/content/92f4e036-6b69-11e5-aca9-d87542bf8673; and Aron Lund, "The Factory: A Glimpse into Syria's War Economy," The Century Foundation, February 21, 2018, https://tcf.org/content/report/factory-glimpse-syrias-war-economy.

265. Isabel Coles, "Despair, Hardship as Iraq Cuts Off Wages in Islamic State Cities," *Reuters*, October 2, 2015, https://www.reuters.com/article/us-mideast-crisis-iraq-salaries/despair-hardship-as-iraq-cuts-off-wages-in-islamic-state-cities-idUSKCN0RW0V620151002.

266. Callimachi, "The ISIS Files."

267. William Rosenau and Zack Gold, "'The Cheapest Insurance in the World?' The United States and Proxy Warfare," CNA Analysis & Solutions, July 2019, https://www.cna.org/CNA_files/PDF/DRM-2019-U-020227-1Rev.pdf.

268. See Dina Esfandiary, "No Country for Oversimplifications," The Century Foundation, January 24, 2018, https://tcf.org/content/report/no-country-oversimplifications/.

269. Ariane Tabatabai and Dina Esfandiary, "Cooperating with Iran to Combat ISIS in Iraq," *Washington Quarterly*, 40, iss. 3 (2017): 134.

270. Afshon Ostovar, "Iran, Its Clients, and the Future of the Middle East: The Limits of Religion," *International Affairs*, 94, no. 6 (2018): 1237–55, 1237.

271. On perceptions of tight control, see Con Coughlin, "Iran Is the Force behind the Houthis. The World Should Hold It to Account," *National*, June 21 2018, https://www.thenational.ae/opinion/comment/iran-is-the-force-behind-the-houthis-the-world-should-hold-it-to-account-1.742825; "Al-Jubeir: Houthi Attack Proves They Are Indivisible Part of IRGC," *Al-Arabiya*, May 16, 2019, https://english.alarabiya.net/en/News/gulf/2019/05/16/Al-Jubeir-Houthi-attack-proves-they-are-indivisible-part-of-IRGC.html; and Anjana Sankar, "UAE Tables Evidence of Iran Involvement in Yemen," *Khaleej Times*, June 20, 2018, https://www.khaleejtimes.com/news/government/uae-recovers-iran-made-weapons/-used-by-houthis-in-yemen-. On the more nuanced reality, see, for example, Dina Esfandiary and Ariane Tabatabai, "Yemen: An Opportunity for Iran-Saudi Dialogue?" *Washington Quarterly* 39, iss. 2 (2016): 155–74; and Narges Bajoghli, "The Hidden Sources of Iranian Strength," *Foreign Policy*, May 15, 2019, https://foreignpolicy.com/2019/05/15/the-hidden-sources-of-iranian-strength/.

272. Prince Khalid bin Salman, "It Is Worth Considering the Abundant and Disturbing Parallels between 2018 and 1938," *Arab News*, July 23, 2018, https://www.memri.org/reports/saudi-ambassador-us-khalid-bin-salman-irans-malign-behavior-must-be-confronted-not-appeased#_edn1.

273. Remarks by Sheikh Khalid bin Ahmed Al Khalifa, Fourteenth Middle East Security Summit, IISS Manama Dialogue, Second Plenary Session, October 27, 2018.

274. "On the Arabian Peninsula," Khalifa said, "Yemen has become the latest casualty of the Islamic Republic of Iran's quest for regional dominance. The Islamic Republic's interference in the affairs of Yemen, and its support to the terrorist Houthi organization, has prolonged the conflict and contributes to the Houthi unwillingness to return to the political process that all Yemeni parties agreed to in 2012 and to abandon their armed rebellion." Ibid.

275. Shams Ahsan, "Houthi Militias a Threat to the Region: Maliki," *Saudi Gazette*, May 31, 2019, http://saudigazette.com.sa/article/567789/SAUDI-ARABIA/ Houthi-militias-a-threat-to-the-region-Maliki; and Mohammed Al-Kinani, "Houthis an 'Arm of Iran that Threatens Yemen's Existence,'" *Arab News*, May 31 2019, http:// www.arabnews.com/node/1504726/middle-east.

276. For more on the concept of Rule of the Jurisprudent, see Imam [Ruholla] Khomeini, *Islamic Government: Governance of the Jurist (Velayat-e-Faqh)*, (Tehran: The Institute for Compilation and Publication of Imam Khomeini's Works—International Affairs Department, 1970).; Hamid Dabashi, *Theology of Discontent: The Ideological Foundation of the Islamic Revolution in Iran* (New Brunswick, CT: Transaction Publishers, 2006); Hossein Seifzadeh, "Ayatollah Khomeini's Concept of Rightful Government: The Valayat-e-Faqih," in *Islam, Muslims and the Modern State*, ed. Hussin Mutalib and Taj ul-Islam Hashmi (London: Palgrave Macmillan, 1994), 197–210; M. Mahtab Alam Rizvi, "Velayat-e-Faqih (Supreme Leader) and Iranian Foreign Policy: An Historical Analysis," *Strategic Analysis* 36, no. 1 (2012): 112–27; and David Menashri, "Ayatollah Khomeini and the Velayat-e-Faqih," in *Militancy and Political Violence in Shiism: Trends and Patterns*, ed. Assaf Moghadam (London: Routledge, 2011).

277. Bruce Riedel, "Who Are the Houthis, and Why Are We at War with Them?" *Markaz*, Brookings, December 18, 2017, https://www.brookings.edu/blog/ markaz/2017/12/18/who-are-the-houthis-and-why-are-we-at-war-with-them/.

278. The Zaydi reject certain beliefs that are fundamental to Iranian Shiism. See Esfandiary and Tabatabai, "Yemen: an Opportunity for Iran-Saudi Dialogue?" 157.

279. Esfandiary and Tabatabai, "Yemen," 157; and Sultan Barakat, "Saudi Arabia's War in Yemen: The Moral Questions," *Markaz*, Brookings, March 31, 2015, https://www.brookings.edu/blog/markaz/2015/03/31/saudi-arabias-war-in-yemen-the-moral-questions/.

280. Esfandiary and Tabatabai, "Yemen," 166.

281. Becca Wasser and Ariane Tabatabai, "Iran's Network of Fighters in the Middle East Aren't Always Loyal to Iran," *Washington Post*, May 21, 2019, https://www.washingtonpost.com/politics/2019/05/21/how-do-irans-proxies-actually-work/.

282. Author interview with senior Iranian official, Berlin, June 26, 2017.

283. Bajoghli, "Hidden Sources of Iranian Strength."

284. Afshon Ostovar, "The Grand Strategy of Militant Clients: Iran's Way of War," *Security Studies* 28, no. 1 (2018): 159–88, 180.

285. "Receiving patronage from Iran further connects the recipient to Iran's antagonisms, the sanctions imposed on it by the UN and the US, and the baggage of its reputation as a state sponsor of terrorism. If a group wants to up-end the status quo, and favors Iran's vision of what should replace it, then the trade-offs of being allied with Tehran might be worth the benefits (financial and military support, loyalty in the face of international pressure, and willingness to partner with extremist militant groups)." Ostovar, "Iran, Its Clients, and the Future of the Middle East," 1248.

286. Michael Wahid Hanna and Dalia Dassa Kaye, "The Limits of Iranian Power," *Survival* 57, no. 5 (2015): 173–98.

287. "Stand Strong in the Face of Saudi & UAE Plots to Divide Yemen: Imam Khamenei," Khameini.ir, August 13, 2019, http://english.khamenei.ir/news/6976/ Stand-strong-in-the-face-of-Saudi-UAE-plots-to-divide-Yemen.

288. Ariane Tabatabai (@ArianeTabatabai), Twitter status, August 13, 2019, https://twitter.com/ArianeTabatabai/status/1161423251668705280.

289. Ostovar, "Iran, Its Clients, and the Future of the Middle East," 1247.

290. Jason Rezaian and Abigail Hauslohner, "Ahmadinejad Makes First Cairo Visit," *Washington Post*, February 5, 2013, ttps://www.washingtonpost.com/world/ middle_east/ahmadinejad-makes-first-cairo-visit/2013/02/05/935b2c68-6fb0-11e2-b35a-0ee56f0518d2_story.html.

291. Statement by Iranian academic, speaking with the expectation of anonymity, roundtable on regional security, Lausanne, December 12, 2017.

292. Statement by Iranian academic, roundtable on regional security, Lausanne.

293. This analysis draws from Tabatabai and Esfandiary, "Cooperating with Iran to Combat ISIS," 137. The Iranian revolutionary-style blend of politics and religion is not popular among Iraq's Shia. Iraqi Shia cleric Grand Ayatollah Abd al-Qasim al-Khoei (1899–1992) thought that religious leaders should not involve themselves in politics, in contrast to the Rule of the Jurisprudent concept that Khomeini promoted. Today, Ayatollah Ali al-Sistani maintains a similar perspective to al-Khoei, rejecting Khomeini's vision.

294. Tabatabai and Esfandiary, "Cooperating with Iran to Combat ISIS," 137; Ranj Alaaldin, "Iran's Weak Grip: How Much Control Does Tehran Have Over Shia Militias in Iraq?" *Foreign Affairs*, February 11, 2016, https://www.foreignaffairs.com/ articles/iran/2016-02-11/irans-weak-grip.

295. Bajoghli, "Hidden Sources of Iranian Strength."

296. See Susannah George, "Breaking Badr," *Foreign Policy*, November 6, 2014, https://foreignpolicy.com/2014/11/06/breaking-badr/. In contrast, as detailed in the case study on the PMU in this report, other PMU members, such as Muqtada al-Sadr's Peace Brigades, are outspoken in their opposition to Iranian intervention.

297. Maher Chmaytelli, "Iranian-Backed Shi'ite Militia Chief Aims to Lead Iraq," Reuters, May 8, 2018, https://www.reuters.com/article/us-iraq-election-amiri/ iranian-backed-shiite-militia-chief-aims-to-lead-iraq-idUSKBN1I91NL.

298. Alex Vatanka, "Iran's Use of Shi'i Militant Proxies—Ideological and Practical Expediency versus Uncertain Sustainability," Middle East Institute Policy Paper no. 5, June 2018, https://www.mei.edu/sites/default/files/publications/Vatanka_ PolicyPaper.pdf, 4.

299. On Hezbollah, see Ze'ev Schiff, "Israel's War with Iran," *Foreign Affairs*, December 4, 2006, https://www.foreignaffairs.com/articles/iran/2006-11-01/ israels-war-iran. On Hamas, see Omar Fahmy and Nidal al-Mughrabi, "Hamas Ditches Assad, Back Syrian Revolt," Reuters, February 24, 2012, https://www.

reuters.com/article/us-syria-palestinians/hamas-ditches-assad-backs-syrian-revolt-idUSTRE81N1CC20120224.

300. Iranian official who wished to remain anonymous, interview with the author.

301. See "U.S. Says Iran Spends $1 Billion Annually on Supporting Terrorism," *Iran Primer*, United States Institute of Peace, November 13, 2018, https://iranprimer.usip.org/index.php/blog/2018/nov/13/us-says-iran-spends-1-billion-annually-supporting-terrorism; and David Adesnik, "Iran Spends $16 Billion Annually to Support Terrorists and Rogue Regimes," FDD Policy Briefs, January 10, 2018, https://www.fdd.org/analysis/2018/01/10/iran-spends-16-billion-annually-to-support-terrorists-and-rogue-regimes/.

302. See Suzanne Maloney, "Major Beneficiaries of the Iran Deal: The IRGC and Hezbollah," Testimony to House Committee on Foreign Affairs Subcommittee on the Middle East and North Africa, published via Brookings, September 17, 2015, https://www.brookings.edu/testimonies/major-beneficiaries-of-the-iran-deal-the-irgc-and-hezbollah/; "The Middle East After the Iran Nuclear Deal," Council on Foreign Relations Expert Roundup, September 3, 2015, https://www.cfr.org/expert-roundup/middle-east-after-iran-nuclear-deal; and Magnus Norell, "A Really Bad Deal: The Iran Nuclear Deal and Its Implications," *European View* 14, no. 2 (2015): 285–91.

303. Even aside from the fact that Iran's assistance to nonstate actors has remained relatively impervious to the country's economic situation, many of the criticisms of the Iran deal were based on inaccuracies and exaggerations. Donald Trump claimed that the deal released $150 billion in assets back to the government, and an additional $1.8 billion in cash. In fact, the deal simply allowed Iran to access its own formerly frozen money, estimates of which vary between $29 billion and $100 billion. Tehran also received $1.7 billion in a cash transfer as payment for the resolution of an arms contract agreed on by the United States and Iran before the 1979 revolution, which was never paid out. See Linda Qiu, "5 Claims from Trump's Speech on Iran Deal That Are Misleading or Need Context," *New York Times*, May 8, 2018, https://www.nytimes.com/2018/05/08/us/politics/trump-fact-check-iran-nuclear-deal.html; Jon Greenberg, "Donald Trump Says Iran Got $150 billion and $1.8 Billion in Cash. That's Half True," *Politifact*, April 27, 2018, https://www.politifact.com/truth-o-meter/statements/2018/apr/27/donald-trump/donald-trump-iran-150-billion-and-18-billion-c/; Richard Nephew, "Sanctions Relief Won't Be a $100 Billion Windfall for Iran's Terrorist Friends," *Foreign Policy*, July 2, 2015, https://foreignpolicy.com/2015/07/02/iran-rouhani-khamenei-syria-assad-nuclear-sanctions-hezbollah/; and "$1.7 Billion Payment to Iran Was All in Cash Due to Effectiveness of Sanctions, White House Says," *Los Angeles Times*, September 7, 2016, https://www.latimes.com/nation/nationnow/la-na-iran-payment-cash-20160907-snap-story.html.

304. Imam Khomeini, *Governance of the Jurist*.

305. Alex Vatanka, "Iran's Use of Shi'i Militant Proxies," 3. For more on the sectarian dimension of Iran's regional policy, see ibid., 3–5.

306. On the military purges, see "Khomeini Orders Military Purge and Increased Pressure on Left," Associated Press, July 10, 1981; and Hooshang Amirahmadi and Manoucher Parvin, *Post-Revolutionary Iran* (New York, Oxon: Routledge, 1988). For more on the Iran-Iraq War and its effects, see Efraim Karsh, *The Iran-Iraq War* (New York: Rosen Publishing, 2009).

307. For more on the IRGC, its place in the Islamic Republic and its rise, see Afshon Ostovar, *Vanguard of the Imam: Religion, Politics and Iran's Revolutionary Guards* (Oxford: Oxford University Press, 2016).

308. "Iran's Revolutionary Guards," Backgrounder, Council on Foreign Relations, May 6, 2019, https://www.cfr.org/backgrounder/irans-revolutionary-guards.

309. Karim Sadjadpour, *Reading Khamenei: The World View of Iran's Most Powerful Leader* (Washington, DC: Carnegie Endowment for International Peace, 2009), 8.

310. "Profile: Iran's Revolutionary Guards," BBC News, April 8, 2019, https://www.bbc.com/news/world-middle-east-47852262.

311. For more on the economic role of the IRGC, see "Economic Expansion: The IRGANC's Business Conglomerate and Public Works," in *The Rise of the Pasdaran: Assessing the Domestic Roles of Iran's Islamic Revolutionary Guards Corps*, ed. Frederic Wehrey, Jerrold D. Green, Brian Nichiporuk, Alireza Nader, Lydia Hansell, Rasool Naf'isi, and S. R. Bohandy (Washington, DC: The RAND Corporation, 2009), 55–75.

312. One example of the IRGC's economic and political strength growing in tandem following sanctions involves the Natanz nuclear fuel enrichment plant, whose existence was revealed in 2002 by the National Council of Resistance, an Iranian opposition group (Tehran had tried to keep it a secret). Following the exposure of the program, the IRGC received authorization from the Ministry of Defense to become involved in the program's infrastructure. As a result, an IRGC-controlled construction firm, Khatam al-Anbia, benefited greatly. See Ahmad Majidyar, "Defying Pressure, Khatam al Anbiya Chief Defends IRGC's Economic Role," Middle East Institute, February 9, 2018, https://www.mei.edu/publications/defying-pressure-khatam-al-anbia-chief-defends-irgcs-economic-role.

313. This division of labor is not codified in Iranian law. Rather, the supreme leader decides which agency is responsible. In Iran, it is accepted that important foreign policy, and especially regional security files, are under the control of the IRGC.

314. Dina Esfandiary and Ariane Tabatabai, "Iran's ISIS Policy," *International Affairs* 91, no. 1 (2015): 2–5.

315. The campaign was also a response to rumors that Soleimani would be replaced. See Joanna Paraszczuk, "Iran's 'Shadow Commander' Steps into the Light," *Atlantic*, October 16, 2014, https://www.theatlantic.com/international/archive/2014/10/irans-shadow-commander-steps-into-the-limelight/381558/; Ostovar, *Vanguard of the Imam*, 226–27; and Narges Bajoghli, "The IRGC's Plan to Win Hearts and Minds," *Al-Monitor*, March 13, 2016, https://www.al-monitor.com/pulse/originals/2016/03/iran-irgc-qassem-soleimani-quds-force-charm-offensive.html.

316. Ostovar, *Vanguard of the Imam,* 226.

317. Dina Esfandiary and Ariane Tabatabai, "A Comparative Study of U.S. and Iranian Counter-ISIS Strategies," *Studies in Conflict & Terrorism* 40, no. 6 (2017): 461.

318. Najmeh Bozorgmehr, "Iran Cracks Down on Revolutionary Guards Business Network," *Financial Times,* September 14, 2017.

319. Lionel Beehner and Greg Bruno, "'Iran's Involvement in Iraq," Backgrounder, Council on Foreign Relations, March 3, 2008, https://www.cfr.org/backgrounder/irans-involvement-iraq.

320. Assistance came in the form of finances, materiel—including weapons and equipment—and military aid, including the provision of intelligence, training, and advice. See Esfandiary and Tabatabai, "Iran's ISIS Policy."

321. Alireza Nader, "Iran's Role in Iraq: Room for Cooperation?" (Washington, DC: RAND Corporation, 2015), 5 http://www.rand.org/pubs/perspectives/PE151.html.

322. For more on these cross-border links, see Salih and Fantappie, "Kurdish Nationalism at an Impasse."

323. Senior Iranian official, interview with author, Lausanne, Switzerland, March 2015.

324. Esfandiary and Tabatabai, "Iran's ISIS policy."

325. For more on Iran's reaction to and policy on combating the Islamic State, see Esfandiary and Tabatabai, "Iran's ISIS Policy."

326. Ariane M. Tabatabai, "Syria Changed the Iranian Way of War," *Foreign Affairs,* August 16, 2019, https://www.foreignaffairs.com/articles/syria/2019-08-16/syria-changed-iranian-way-war.

327. For more on the Fatemiyoun Brigade, see Tobias Schneider, "The Fatemiyoun Division: Afghan Fighters in the Syrian Civil War," Middle East Institute Policy Paper, October 2018, https://www.mei.edu/sites/default/files/2018-11/PP11_Schneider.pdf.

328. Mariam Karouny, "Shi'ite Fighters Rally to Defend Damascus Shrine," Reuters, March 3, 2013, https://www.reuters.com/article/us-syria-crisis-shiites/shiite-fighters-rally-to-defend-damascus-shrine-idUSBRE92202X20130303.

329. Ali Alfoneh, "Iraqi Shia Fighters in Syria," Syria Source, Atlantic Council, May 4, 2017, https://www.atlanticcouncil.org/blogs/syriasource/iraqi-shia-fighters-in-syria.

330. Nizar Latif, "Resentment Grows towards Tehran," *National,* June 1, 2009, https://www.thenational.ae/world/mena/resentment-grows-towards-tehran-1.532926; Michael Georgy, "Fiery Cleric Sadr Taps Anger over Iran to Lead Iraq Poll," Reuters, May 14, 2018, https://www.reuters.com/article/us-iraq-election-sadr/fiery-cleric-sadr-taps-anger-over-iran-to-lead-iraq-poll-idUSKCN1IF2G8; and Faris Omran, "Iraqis Resent Iran's Interference in Their Affairs," *Diyaruna,* February 20, 2019, https://diyaruna.com/en_GB/articles/cnmi_di/features/2019/02/20/feature-01.

331. As Vatanka puts it, Iran's ability to succeed in the future will depend on "the willingness of Arab groups to continue to be subservient to the IRGC (Iranian) agenda, and the tolerance level of the Iranian public to see the IRGC continue its military adventurism in the region despite the risks and costs it entails." Vatanka, "Iran's Use of Shi'i Militant Proxies," 13.

332. Ostovar, "The Grand Strategy of Militant Clients," 180.

333. As the scholar Daniel Byman argues, "At times, the greatest contribution a state can make to a terrorist's cause is to simply not act against it." Daniel Byman, *Deadly Connections: States that Sponsor Terrorism* (New York: Cambridge University Press, 2005), 219.

334. Joby Warrick, "Private Donations Give Edge to Islamists in Syria, Officials Say," *Washington Post*, September 21, 2013, https://www.washingtonpost.com/world/national-security/private-donations-give-edge-to-islamists-in-syria-officials-say/2013/09/21/a6c783d2-2207-11e3-a358-1144dee636dd_story.html.

335. The Nusra Front was first established in Syria by the Islamic State of Iraq and then designated as a terrorist group in December 2012. See Aron Lund, "The Non-State Militant Landscape in Syria," *CTC Sentinel* 6, no. 8 (2013): https://ctc.usma.edu/the-non-state-militant-landscape-in-syria/.

336. One early such example was Ahrar al-Sham's early rejection of the "'regionalization' of the Syrian war," which was understood as a reference to the transnational project of other Islamist groups, such as Nusra. Ibid.

337. Ostovar, "The Grand Strategy of Militant Clients," 180.

338. Ostovar, "Iran, Its Clients, and the Future of the Middle East," 1241.

339. "Exploiting Disorder: Al-Qaeda and the Islamic State," International Crisis Group, March 14, 2016, https://www.crisisgroup.org/global/exploiting-disorder-al-qaeda-and-islamic-state.

340. Ibid.

341. Mansour and Salisbury, "Between Order and Chaos."

342. Ibid.

343. Ibid.

About the Authors

Thanassis Cambanis is a senior fellow at The Century Foundation, specializing in the Middle East and U.S. foreign policy. He is the author of *Once Upon a Revolution: An Egyptian Story* (Simon and Schuster, 2015) and *A Privilege to Die: Inside Hezbollah's Legions and Their Endless War against Israel* (Free Press, 2010).

Dina Esfandiary is a fellow at The Century Foundation and international security program research fellow at Harvard's Kennedy School. She is the co-author *of Triple-Axis: Iran's Relations with Russia and China* (London: I. B. Tauris, 2018), and *Living on the Edge: Iran and the Practice of Nuclear Hedging* (Palgrave Macmillan, 2016).

Sima Ghaddar is a doctoral student in sociology at the University of California, Los Angeles where she studies state formation. She was previously a policy associate at The Century Foundation in Beirut.

Michael Wahid Hanna is a senior fellow at The Century Foundation. He is also a nonresident senior fellow at the Reiss Center on Law and Security at New York University School of Law. Hanna works on issues of international security, international law, and U.S. foreign policy in the Middle East and South Asia.

Aron Lund is a fellow at The Century Foundation and a guest researcher at the Stockholm International Peace Research Institute. He has published two Swedish-language books on Syrian politics, *Drömmen om Damaskus* [The Dream of Damascus] (Stockholm, 2010) and *Syrien brinner* [Syria Is Burning] (Stockholm, 2014), and the English-language *Divided They Stand: An Overview of Syria's Political Opposition Factions* (Brussels, 2012). In 2018 and 2019, his work was supported by a grant from the Harry Frank Guggenheim Foundation.

Renad Mansour is a research fellow in the Middle East and North Africa Programme at Chatham House. He is also a research fellow at the Cambridge Security Initiative based at Cambridge University, and a research fellow at the Institute of Regional and International Studies at the American University of Iraq, Sulaimani. He received his PhD from Cambridge University.

www.ingramcontent.com/pod-product-compliance
Lightning Source LLC
Chambersburg PA
CBHW041257040426
42334CB00028BA/3048